RSAC

D0734764

BOOK

WAS

THERE

BOOK

Reading in Electronic Times

WAS

Andrew Piper

THERE

The University of Chicago Press   CHICAGO + LONDON

ANDREW PIPER teaches German and European literature at
McGill University and is the author of *Dreaming in Books*,
also published by the University of Chicago Press.

The University of Chicago Press, Chicago 60637
The University of Chicago Press, Ltd., London
© 2012 by The University of Chicago
All rights reserved. Published 2012.
Printed in the United States of America

21 20 19 18 17 16 15 14 13 12   1 2 3 4 5

ISBN-13: 978-0-226-66978-6 (cloth)
ISBN-13: 978-0-226-92289-8 (e-book)
ISBN-10: 0-226-66978-5 (cloth)
ISBN-10: 0-226-92289-8 (e-book)

Library of Congress Cataloging-in-Publication Data

Piper, Andrew, 1973– author.
Book was there : reading in electronic times / Andrew Piper.
pages cm
Includes bibliographical references.
ISBN-13: 978-0-226-66978-6 (cloth: alkaline paper)
ISBN-10: 0-226-66978-5 (cloth: alkaline paper)
ISBN-13: 978-0-226-92289-8 (e-book)
ISBN-10: 0-226-92289-8 (e-book)
1. Books and reading. 2. Reading—Technological
innovations. I. Title.
Z1003.P576 2012
028.9—dc23
2012004868

♾ This paper meets the requirements of ANSI/NISO
Z39.48-1992 (Permanence of Paper).

CONTENTS

Nothing Is Ever New

Book was there, it was there.

GERTRUDE STEIN

When I was punished as a child, I was sent to my room to read. You won't find this in many parenting handbooks today. From this I learned that reading was an activity that allowed me to calm down, to locate a sense of repose, which was not that easy for an eight-year-old boy with an older brother. It was the first intimation I had, unconscious at the time, that reading was a discipline. It takes work to learn, to advance, to maintain. Reading isn't just an escape, it also disciplines us, it molds us into who we are. I am now, thanks to my disciplinary past, a professor of literature.

I was not just a reader as a child, but also a computer user. I belong to the first generation of children who grew up using personal computers. We had a Radio Shack TRS-80 at home (and Pong), a Commodore 64 at school, and later an Apple IIe on which I wrote my college applications. I was programming my TRS-80 when I was nine. I went to computer camp. Computers and video games were as much a part of my life as books.

Personal tales of readers are often shaded by a touch of hyperbole: Goethe tells us he had read all of Racine and Molière by the age of nine, Sartre tells us he had finished the encyclopedia before most children had begun reading, that sort of thing. Great readers have always read all of the books. By this definition, I was never a great reader. Maybe that's why I had to be sent to my room. Or maybe it was all those electronic gadgets vying for my attention, or maybe it was too many reruns of *Three's Company*. It is too hard to say now. For me, the book was never the superhero of most readers' personal histories. But it was at least still there.

Today, my children, who are now four and seven, are growing up in a world where this balance seems to many to be coming unhinged. We worry that these new "digital natives" will never know what it is like to sit in a room of their own and read a book. They won't share my memories of the punctuated stillness and the contoured sensuality of turning the pages of Shel Silverstein, *The Wind in the Willows*, or the mind-bending work of Madeleine L'Engle. All they will know is the frenetic, problem-solving interactivity of the electronic screen. As a last ditch effort to instill in them an attachment to the book, my wife and I now take away story time when our children are punished (this too you will likely not find in today's parenting handbooks). But for how much longer can the book seem like a forbidden fruit?

For some, however, we are not doing *enough* interacting with our digital devices. We know how to play with them, but few understand anymore how they work. Knowledge of our reading tools is lagging behind our use of them. They have become the ultimate black boxes, functional (mostly) and sealed off from human understanding. We are becoming the tools of our machines and not the other way around. In this sense, we are becoming less and less literate.

As both a parent and a professor, my job is to teach young people how to read. However far apart these two audiences may seem—one group is learning to decode narrative structure, the other the shape of letters—they are connected by belonging to the same trajectory of how reading informs who we are and how we think. And never before has this trajectory, for children and adults alike, seemed more unsettled due to changes in the material, not content, of what we read. Trying to understand how technologies, both new and old, shape how we read has emerged as one of the more urgent concerns of my personal and professional life. Judging by the amount of material written on the subject of late, it clearly has for many others, too. Answers are both too plentiful and too premature right now. What we really need is a better road map.

+ +

This book is not a case for or against books. It is not about old media or new media (or even new new media). Instead, it is an attempt to understand the relationship between books and screens, to identify some of their fundamental differences and to chart out the continuities that might run between them. Much like my own personal history in which computers and books were interwoven into the fabric of my life from the very start, electronic reading has a very deep bibliographic history. In Gertrude Stein's words, books were there. It is this thereness that is both essential for understanding the medium of the book (that books exist as finite objects in the world) and also for reminding us that we cannot think about our electronic future without contending with its antecedent, the bookish past. Books got there first. Books and screens are now bound up with one another whether we like it or not. Only in patiently working through this entanglement will we be able to understand how new technologies will, or will not, change how we read. I can imagine a world without books. I cannot imagine one without reading.

There is by now a vast field of research that falls under the heading of reading.[1] But in truth we have no idea what happens when people read. People have read out loud, silently, linearly, haphazardly, attentively, distractedly, purposefully, together or alone, with or without pens or pencils, with one hand or two, while sitting, reclining, standing, or walking, by candlelight, sunlight, or even moonlight. People have slept while appearing to read, read while appearing to sleep (children and flashlights!), and left books lying around as though they might be read soon or someday or never. Reading is a way of disciplining our minds, and it is also one of the most efficient means of mental escape. More recently, thanks to the wonders of new imaging technologies, we have learned how the mind and the eye work together to process words on the page (by making four to five jumps every second) and whether we decode words phonetically or graphically (the answer is both). We now have scholarly databases to record our reading experiences—if reading's soporific rhythms can indeed be called an "experience"—and courtesy of electronic readers, organizations can aggregate users' page views and note taking so that we, or some of us, can see the sum total of readers' habits.

Despite all of this we really have no idea what it is people do when they read. That is one of reading's great gifts to ourselves— the creation of a practice that is fundamentally opaque. To think of doing something that could be impossible to define or to know—the ultimate human daring. First came fire, then text.

And yet. Things ask us to do certain things with them. Things are not unconditional. We may do what we please with books or screens (use them as doorstops, drop them in sinks), but they still shape our access to what we read and how we construct our mental universes through them. Whether it is the soft graininess of the page or the resistant slickness of the screen, the kinetic activities of swiping instead of turning, the postural differences of sitting back versus up, tilting our heads down or forward, grasping with our hands or resting our hands on, the shape of folded sheets versus the roamable, zoomable, or clickable surfaces of the electronic screen—all of these features (and many more) contribute to a different relationship to reading, and thus thinking. Things help us think and thereby contribute to the shape of our thoughts. The shape of reading, what it has been and what it might be, is what this book is about.

Much ink has been spilled (whether electronic or the oily kind) on the topic of the future of the book. Every day someone somewhere says that the end of the book is nigh, that young people only read online (like Gautier said of the Romantics and the Italian Army: they are always young), that we're killing too many trees, that, really, what's the difference?[2] And then right after that someone will say the Internet is making us stupider, twitchier, addicted, and perhaps worst of all, bad spellers.[3] We take little notice that we have said all this before. Four hundred years ago in Spain people read too many romances (Don Quixote), three hundred years ago in London too many people wrote crap (Grub Street), two hundred years ago in Germany reading had turned into a madness (the so-called *Lesewut*), and one hundred years ago there was the telephone. We have worried that one day there would be more authors than readers (in 1788), that self-publishing would save, and then kill, reading (in 1773), and that no one would have time to read books anymore (in 1855).[4] Everything that has been said about life in an online world has already been said about books.

Books will always be there. That is what they are by definition: there. Whether in the classroom, the library, the archive, the bookstore, the warehouse, or online, it is our choice, however, *where* books will be. It is time to stop worrying and start thinking. It is time to put an end to the digital utopias and print eulogies, bookish venerations and network gothic, and tired binaries like deep versus shallow, distributed versus linear, or slow versus fast. Now is the time to understand the rich history of what we have thought books have done for us and what we think digital texts might do differently. We need to remember the diversity that surrounds reading and the manifold, and sometimes strange, tools upon which it has historically been based. The question is not one of "versus," of two single antagonists squaring off in a ring; rather, the question is far more ecological in nature.[5] How will these two very different species and their many varieties coexist within the greater ecosystem known as reading?

The study of the book's past has thankfully, and perhaps not unsurprisingly, undergone a renaissance of late. Once relegated to the academic backwaters known as "publishing history," it is now at the forefront of numerous different disciplines. There are multivolume handbooks on the history of the book in the West, in the world, in general, and individually by country.[6] There are centers for the study of the book in Edinburgh, Princeton, Toronto, and Hong Kong, and "book arts" has become a popular new graduate degree. There is nothing like a sense of demise to spur our attention.

At the same time of course, there is a booming industry in the study of new media. Once the domain of intellectuals who seemingly never grew up, universities are now tripping over themselves to establish the institutional infrastructure for the study of digital life. And yet seldom are these two worlds in conversation with one another in any meaningful sense. Historians of the book who stray into the fields of digital media are disciplined by accusations of anachronism. Media historians who stray into the world of books are threatened with irrelevance.[7] This book attempts to bridge that divide. In the spirit of my own past, it is decidedly stereoscopic.

Unlike the jeremiad, the manifesto, or the multivolume handbook, however, what you have in your hands is something far more personal as well as diminutive (though I have tried in the notes to give readers an introduction into the various fields of research that the book covers). *Book Was There* is more akin to an essay in the classical sense, an "attempt" to understand how reading is beginning to change—for myself, for my students, and of course for my children. It's this latter group whom I was thinking of most while I wrote this book: my son's strange love of catalogs; my daughter's swift intimation that Charlotte (the spider) was doomed from the moment she appeared on the page; the rapt attention that any screen can command for both of them; and the mysterious difficulty that is the punctuation mark. Along with more famous readers of the past and present, my children too will be making an appearance here. If there is something sentimental about this, it is at least partially because this is the way we've come to understand reading. Ever since the eighteenth century, which after all invented the idea of sentimentality, reading has been integral to our sense of both personal and political development. Getting reading wrong is framed as a threat to who we can *become*, whether as individuals or a society. To talk about reading is always implicitly to talk about the future and the past simultaneously. This is one of the primary reasons why debates about reading become so heated, and why they ultimately, always, come back to "the kids," whether real or our imagined inner child. Wrestling with reading is a way of reflecting on who we once were and who we want to be.

This book is personal in another sense though, one that I think has largely been missing in the many books on the topic of reading's past and future. Each of the chapters is organized around something that we *do* when we read: how we touch books and screens, how we look at them, how we share them with each other, how we take notes with them or navigate our way through them, where we use them, or even how we play with them. In this, I am interested in understanding how we relate to reading in a deeply embodied way.[8] Reading is not only a matter of our brains. It is an integral part of our lived experience, our sense of being in the world, even if at times this can mean feeling intensely apart from the world. We do not as yet have a survey of reading that takes reading quite so experientially seriously as this one.

These are the categories through which I hope we will continue to debate the future of reading. Only when we understand the differences between books and screens at these most elementary of levels—at the level of person, habit, and gesture—can we make informed choices about the values associated with the kind of reading we care about and the technological (and pedagogical) infrastructures that should support such values. Technologies don't just happen. At least not yet. We are still agents in this story, and we have some choices to make. This book is aimed at helping us make an informed choice. It is about moving away from questions of futurology to ones of meaning. Book was there, yes, but what did it mean? And what does it mean still?

ONE

Take It and Read

What I must chiefly remember *are the hands.*
DELACROIX [*diary,* april 11, 1824]

...we were / hands, / we bailed the darkness out...
PAUL CELAN ["flower"]

The meaning of the book could begin with St. Augustine. In the eighth book of his *Confessions*, Augustine describes the moment of his conversion to becoming a Christian:

> In my misery I kept crying, "How long shall I go on saying, 'tomorrow, tomorrow?'" Why not now? Why not make an end of my ugly sins at this very moment? I was asking myself these questions when all at once I heard the singing voice of a child in a nearby house. Whether it was the voice of a boy or girl I cannot say, but again and again it repeated the refrain, "Take it and read, take it and read."

Augustine is sitting beneath a fig tree in his garden, and upon hearing the voice he takes up the Bible lying near him and opens a passage at random and begins reading (Romans 13:13–14). At this moment, he tells us, "I had no wish to read more and no need to do so. For in an instant, as I came to the end of the sentence, it was as though the light of confidence flooded into my heart and all the darkness of doubt was dispelled."[1] Augustine closes the book, marking his place with his finger, and goes to tell his friend Alypius about his experience. His conversion is complete.

No other passage has more profoundly captured the meaning of the book than this one. Not just reading but reading *books* was aligned in Augustine with the act of personal conversion. Augustine was writing at the end of the fourth century, when the codex had largely superseded the scroll as the most prevalent form of reading material.[2] We know Augustine was reading a book from the way he randomly accesses a page and uses his finger to mark his place. The conversion at the heart of *The Confessions* was an affirmation of the new technology of the book within the lives of individuals, indeed, as the technology that helped turn readers *into* individuals. Turning the page, not turning the handle of the scroll, was the new technical prelude to undergoing a major turn in one's own life.

In aligning the practice of book reading with that of personal conversion, Augustine established a paradigm of reading that would far exceed its theological framework, one that would go on to become a foundation of Western humanistic learning for the next fifteen hundred years. It was above all else the graspability of the book, its being "at hand," that allowed it to play such a pivotal role in shaping one's life. "Take it and read, take it and read" (*tolle lege, tolle lege*), repeats the divine refrain. The book's graspability, in a material as well as a spiritual sense, is what endowed it with such immense power to radically alter our lives. In taking hold of the book, according to Augustine, we are taken hold of by books.

Nothing is more suspect today than the book's continued identity of being "at hand." The spines, gatherings, threads, boards, and folds that once gave a book its shapeliness, that fit it to our hands, are being supplanted by the increasingly fine strata of new reading devices, integrated into vast woven systems of connection. If books are essentially vertebral, contributing to our sense of human uniqueness that depends upon bodily uprightness, digital texts are more like invertebrates, subject to the laws of horizontal gene transfer and nonlocal regeneration. They, like jellyfish or hydra polyps, always elude our grasp in some funda-mental sense. What this means for how we read—and how we are taken hold of by what we read—is still far from clear.

Aristotle regarded touch as the most elementary sense. It is how we begin to make our way in the world, to map it, measure it, and make sense of it. Touch is the most self-reflexive of senses, an insight affirmed by the German researcher David Katz, who established the field of touch studies in the early twentieth cen-tury based on his work with World War I amputees.[3] Through the feeling of touch, we learn to feel ourselves. Touch is a form of redundancy, enfolding more sensory information into what we see and therefore what we read. It makes the words on the page richer in meaning and more multidimensional. It gives words a geometry, but also a reflexive quality.

To think about the future of reading means, first and foremost, to think about the relationship between reading and hands, the long history of how touch has shaped reading and, by exten-sion, our sense of ourselves while we read. After completing his early masterpiece *Dante and Virgil*, the great French Romantic painter Eugène Delacroix wrote in his journal, "What I must chiefly remember *are the hands*."[4] As Delacroix said of painting, so too of reading.

+ +

Ever since its inception as a pair of wood boards bearing wax tablets bound together by a loose string, the book has served as a tool of reflection. There is a doubleness to the book that is central to its meaning as an object. With the pages facing each other as they face us, the open book stands before us as a mirror. But even when closed, the book is still informed by a basic duality. The grasped book is not only a sign of openness and accessibility, as it was for Augustine. It can also be an affront, closing something (or someone) off in the name of opening something up.

Consider Adolf von Menzel's *Man Holding a Book* (fig. 1.1), one of the most sensuous depictions of the relationship between

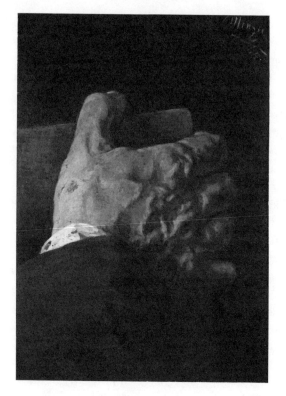

[FIGURE 1.1]   Adolf von Menzel, *Man Holding a Book* (1864).
Courtesy of bpk, Berlin/Nationalgalerie, Staatliche Museen, Berlin,
Germany. Photo: Bernd Kuhnert/Art Resource, New York.

a hand and a book I have ever seen. In it we see the grasping hand
almost entirely consume the image, excluding the man named in
the title from view, but also the book—*so that we cannot even be
sure it is a book anymore.* Grasping closes in the name of reopen-
ing. For Augustine to reopen himself to the world, anew, he must
first close himself off from the world by opening his book. Books
are objects that conjoin openness and closure together, like the
hands to which they belong.

   Nowhere is this more the case than when we read. When we
hold books while we read, our hands are also open. Reading

books, and this is no accident, mimics the gestures of greeting and prayer. In the Middle Ages, this marriage of reading and prayer was combined in one of the most popular book formats from the period, the diminutive "book of hours," which individuals— those who could afford them—carried around with them as daily reminders of religious song and wisdom. In Jean de France, Duc de Berry's *Belles Heures* (1405–8), one of the most lusciously illustrated examples of the genre (fig. 1.2), we see the patron's wife with her hands in prayer before the book. The mirroring that transpires between her hands is then mirrored again in the medium of the open book before her, which is itself mirrored in the figure of God, who is depicted as a trinity grasping a book, the book of the world (although with four, not six, hands, as two are presumably reserved for holding the three of them together). Reading books, we are shown, is expansive, as well as inclusive. It is an act of calling out beyond ourselves, but it is also a symbol of reciprocity: in holding books, we are held together. Every time we hold a book today we are reenacting this initial bond between reading and prayer.

The open hand was the preferred sign of divine calling in both ancient and medieval art.[5] Unable to be present, God spoke through his hand. We do not just call out with books, in other words, but are also called to. The open hand is a reminder that when we read books we hear voices, another sign of the book's essential doubleness. The seventeenth-century physician John Bulwer, who wrote one of the first studies of hand gestures, noted that the hand "speaks all languages." It is in many ways a truer form of speech. As Bulwer writes,

The Tongue and Heart th' intention oft divide:
The Hand and Meaning are ever ally'de.[6]

The book's handiness is a sign of its reliability. Unlike tongues and hearts, books are things that can be trusted, a fact that has much to do with the nature of their tactility.

In the Codex Manesse (1304), one of the most comprehensive

[FIGURE 1.2] Limbourg Brothers (Herman, Pol, and Jean), *The Belles Heures of Jean de France, Duc de Berry*, fol. 91v (1405–8). Image © The Metropolitan Museum of Art, New York.

illustrated books of medieval German love songs, we see how the open hand speaks here too, but this time in the form of the scroll, a common medieval device (fig. 1.3). As a sign of speech, the scroll holds medieval readers (and listeners) together. The scroll (old media) communicates what the book (new media) cannot. Reliability is a function of redundancy, of saying something twice. The use of multiple channels—speech, scroll, book—is the best guarantee that a message will be received, that individuals will arrive at a sense of shared meaning. Like the book's ability to conjoin the different faculties of touch, sight, and sound into a single medium, according to the tradition of the Codex Manesse the book itself is imagined to reside within a more diverse ecology of information. When we think about media death, about the idea of the end of certain technologies, we do well to remember this medieval insistence on the need for redundancy, the importance of communicating the same thing through different channels.

Hands in books do not just speak, they also point in a more literal sense, like Augustine's finger that was used as a bookmark. Books, like hands, *hold* our attention. As early as the twelfth century, writers began drawing hands in the margins of their books to point to important passages.[7] Such a device gradually passed into typescript and became a commonplace of printed books. It looked like this: ☞. The pointing hand in the book stood for the way books themselves were like pointers, making the world graspable. If books open us out into the world, they also constrain. They bring the world down to size, inoculations against the problem of patternlessness.

The child's first drawing is often of his or her own hand. The footprint may be the first mark we make in the world (for hospital records), but the handprint is the original sign of self-reflection, of understanding ourselves as being in the world. The "handbook" or "manual"—the book that reduces the world into its essential parts, into outline form—is an extension of this art of measurement. It is one of the oldest types of books, dating back to Epictetus's *Enchiridion* (second century AD), a short repository of nuggets of wisdom. In the eighth century, the Venerable

[FIGURE 1.3]   Image of the poet Graf Otto von Botenlauben,
who is entrusting his *Minnesang*, or love song, to a young
courier. From Codex Manesse (1304), Cod. Pal. Germ. 848,
fol. 27v. Courtesy of the Universitätsbibliothek Heidelberg.

Bede taught readers to count to a million on their hands in his *On the Reckoning of Time* (AD 725). By the fifteenth and sixteenth centuries, the measuring hand would become the ultimate sign of our bibliographic relationship to the world, embodied in the new genre of the atlas. In its first incarnation, Abraham Ortelius's *Theatrum Orbis Terrarum* (1570), the entire world could now be held in the reader's hand. The secular bravura on display in these books, where the reader assumed the divine view, cannot be overstated. The book was no longer simply a mirror, but a container and a lens at once. By the seventeenth century, the great age of wars of religion, palmistry and chiromancy, knowledge of and on the hand, would become major sciences.[8] Handbooks seem to proliferate in periods of intellectual and technological uncertainty, much as they are proliferating today.

In the nineteenth century, readers witnessed the birth of reading *as* touch, in the form of Louis Braille's invention of a dot-matrix reading system for the blind in 1824. The method derived from an earlier request by Napoleon for a code that could be read by his soldiers at night in the field without the use of light. Braille's innovation was to make the dot-matrix representation of letters small enough to correspond to a single touch of the finger. It made reading digital in a very literal sense. By the end of the century, libraries such as the National Library for the Blind in Britain contained over eight thousand volumes in braille, one of many subsequent technologies that aimed to bring reading to the visually impaired.

The turn of the twentieth century was a period of numerous experiments with the tactility of reading, both practical and impractical, culminating in the modernist revival of experimental books between the world wars.[9] Books made of sandpaper, cardboard, cheap notebook paper, wood, and even metal were some of the many ways that artists experimented with the touch of reading. In the Russian artist El Lissitzky's celebrated *Architecture of VKhUTEMAS* (1927) (fig. 1.4), we see how the disembodied hand of the divine voice from the medieval book has returned, now in the form of the drafting hand of modern science. With

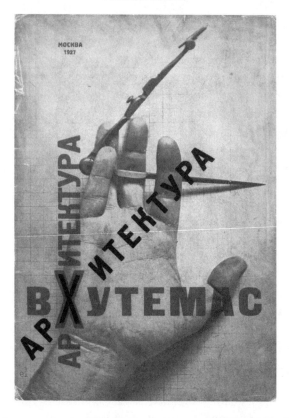

[FIGURE 1.4]   El Lissitzky, *Architecture of VKhUTEMAS*
(1927). © Estate of El Lissitzky/SODRAC (2011). Image courtesy
of the Collection Centre Canadien d'architecture/Canadian
Centre for Architecture, Montreal, Quebec, Canada.

the compass needle seemingly woven into the hand's grip, we
can see Lissitzky performing a subtle visual pun. The compass
needle is imagined to stand in for the sewing needle, one of the
original tools of bookmaking through the sewn binding of the
book's spine. For the Russian avant-garde, the rectilinearity of
modernism—the cube, plane, column, grid—was as much born
from the book as it was the industrial Gargantua of the new machine age. The handbook was one of modernism's secret muses.

If the book's handiness has been fundamental to the way we have taken stock of the world, its ability to serve as a *container* has been another way through which we have found order in our lives. Books are things that hold things. They are proxies for our hands, much like the popular device of the clasp, which was initially used to keep the pages of books from expanding in the humidity.[10] The book's meaning is tied to the way it relates, in an encapsulating way, to other objects in our lives. Scrapbooks—the books that record the sediments of our reading—are an integral part of the history of the book.[11] But so too are wallet bindings, introduced in the fifteenth century, which allow readers to place objects in a special front pocket, like pencils, eyeglasses, or notes, but also things like flowers and artificial flies (for fishing), as in *The Companion to Alfred Ronald's Fly Fisher's Entomology* (1836), which contains hundreds of flies hooked into its pages. Musical records, too, began to be tucked into the front pockets of books, as in the popular series Bubble Books That Sing from the 1920s. The trajectory of the "pocket book" from something that fit into your pocket to a book that had its own pockets to becoming a fashionable handbag is marvelous and strange and one deserving of its own history.

Things in books not only draw us into a broader world of everyday objects. They also show us how things impress us, the way *pressure* is an integral component of human knowledge, one that is deeply tactile in its origins. Pressing flowers between the pages of books, a popular activity through the ages for amateurs and experts alike, was not only a means of preserving specimens. It was a way of reflecting on how nature too could leave impressions behind to be read, one more link in the sturdy chain of the long-standing idea of "the book of nature." In the nineteenth century, the Austrian printer Alois Auer pioneered a technique of "self-printing nature," in which specimens were imprinted directly onto soft metal plates and from there inked and printed directly onto the page.[12] It led to a beautiful series, Nature Printed, by the Englishman Henry Bradbury, in which he printed the ferns and other plants of Great Britain directly from real specimens. Nature was thought to reveal herself more transparently through the medium of print. Grasping, measuring, and pressing—these are the activities through which things become *legible* in a bookish world.

But not for everyone. For some readers, the book is anything but graspable. It embodies an act of letting go, losing control, *handing over*. "Without me, little book, you will go into the city," runs Ovid's famous saying about his writing. Books cross time and space; they transcend the individual's grasp. In this, we cannot know what will happen to them when they leave our hands. "Every poem is a betrayal," Goethe once said.[13] Turning over the book to another involves the possibility of losing control of one's meaning, of potentially being betrayed by the reader. As an object that can fit easily into our hands, but also our pockets, the book and its meaning are always potentially purloined.[14] It lends a whole new meaning to the divine command "take it and read."

For those who see in books something meant to circulate, possessing books, holding on to them too tightly, is an indication of a potential mania. The book as object becomes *too* important; it stops being read. "The bibliophile approaches the book with a looking glass," writes the Romantic bookman Charles Nodier, "and the bibliomaniac with a ruler."[15] The private library is not only a refuge of reading; it can also be an asylum. This is what Edgar Allen Poe thought with the invention of his murderous narrator in "Berenice," who says of the family library, "In that chamber I was born."[16] The library, the place of books, is also the potential birthplace of obsessions. It is where we become possessed by our possessions. In Goethe's greatest life's work, *Faust*, which means "fist" in German, the quintessential modern hero famously flees his book-lined study at the opening of the tragedy. Possessing books, holding on to books, can keep us from life. It is a point viscerally illustrated in Anselm Kiefer's *Population Census* (1991), a library that consists of giant lead census tracts, part of a long tradition of big books, from Kandinsky's iron books to Hanno Rauterberg's recent creation for the Holocaust Memorial in Berlin, which consists of two concrete slabs in the shape of a book weighing over six and a half pounds. For Kiefer, these monstrous books, and by extension the vastness of our entire bibliographic past, *cannot* be grasped, inhuman in their immensity and poisonous nature.

This then is the pathological knot of the book, the joint where hands grasp and let go. The grasping hand is not just about proximity and understanding, it is also about arresting and being arrested. To hold on to books is to hold on to time. One of the most popular book formats of the nineteenth century—the twilight of our bookish world—were literary almanacs with titles like *The Keepsake, The Forget-Me-Not, The Souvenir*. These books were designed as gifts, to be handed over so as never to be let go of again (although they were in fact often regifted). They were filled with inscriptions from a parent to a child, a husband to a wife, or an aunt to a niece, and occasionally poems written on the tissue paper between illustrations. In this way readers learned to preserve each other in their books. Books are how we speak with the distant and the dead. That the past lives on in books is a commonplace. The important point is that we can close books—and thus our relationship to the past.

+ +

How can we hold, and hold on to, our digital texts today?

It is not surprising that one of the most canonized pieces of new media art is Camille Utterback and Romy Achituv's *Text Rain* (fig. 1.5), where letters rain down a screen and come to rest on projections of viewers' open hands, one of many new electronic works that take the hand as their conceptual starting point.[17] *Text Rain* is a potent reminder of the way the digital, at least in English, is named after the hand's component parts. The book's handiness is recycled on the screen, only now the circuit that once enclosed us within a larger sense of self and place has become purely solipsistic: we see *ourselves* collecting words with our hands, as we become the new gods. But unlike Duc de Berry's God who could grasp the book of the world in his (many) hands,

[FIGURE 1.5] Camille Utterback and Romy Achituv, *Text Rain* (1999). Interactive installation (custom software, video camera, computer, projector, and lighting), 1.5′ × 10′ projection, 10′ × 20′ interaction area. Image courtesy of the artists.

the words of *Text Rain* can never truly be grasped by our hands. They are like Platonic forms. They remind us how fragile our hold over words is, that we are only ever godlike.

For Augustine, the book's closedness—that it could be grasped as a totality—was integral to its success in generating transformative reading experiences. Digital texts, by contrast, are radically open in their networked form. They are marked by a very weak sense of closure. Indeed, it is often hard to know what to call them (e-books, books, texts, or just documents) without any clear sense of the material differences between them.

But on another level we could say that digital texts don't so much cancel the book's closedness as reinscribe it within themselves. Where books are closed on the outside and open on the inside, digital texts put this relationship in reverse order. The openness of the digital text—that it is hard to know where its contours are—contrasts with a performed inaccessibility that also belongs to the networked text. There is always something "out of touch" about the digital. Consider Kenneth Goldsmith's online *Soliloquy* (2001), which was initially published as a printed book consisting of transcripts of his digitally recorded speech over the course of a single week. In the online version, words on the screen only appear when touched by the cursor (the electronic finger) and then only one sentence at a time. Every time we move the cursor to illuminate another sentence, the one before it disappears, just as the one after remains invisible. Like a jellyfish, the textual whole slips through our fingers.[18]

This is not to imply that digital texts are not at some level "there." This would be to fall prey to the "virtual fallacy" (computing culture's equivalent to Ruskin's "pathetic fallacy"). Digital texts are somewhere, but *where* they are has become increasingly complicated, abstract, even forbidden.[19] If the book is a thing you can put things into, the electronic book keeps things out. We cannot see, let alone finger, the source of the screen's letters, the electromagnetically charged "hard drive," without destroying it, though we can, in a telling reversal of fortune, touch our software. Unlike books, we cannot feel the impressions of the digital. As Shelley Jackson writes in her hypertext fiction, *My Body*, "A blind person could trace my drawing with her fingertips three pages down in my notebooks."[20] The touch of the page brings us into the world (three pages down), while the screen keeps us out. Digital texts lack feeling. All that remains of the hand is a ghostly remnant of its having been there at the time of scanning, like the chance encounters with scanners' hands from Google Books (fig. 1.6), accidental traces of the birth of the digital record. The hand no longer points, like the typographic manicule, it covers over or gets in the way. Hand was there, we might say.

But digital texts *can* be grasped, you will say (I, too, own an e-reader or two). Touch has emerged as one of the most important new fields in contemporary computing.[21] Falling under the heading of "haptics" (like optics for the hand), it encompasses the

[FIGURE I.6]   Scanner's hand from Google Books.
Dedication page of Honoré de Balzac, *Scènes de la vie de
province* (Paris: Charpentier, 1850). Courtesy of Google.

development of touch screens, virtual handshakes, and surgical
training at a distance. But it is also part of a culture of the "handheld," the way computing has steadily been migrating from large
rooms to our desks to our hands. The more screenish our world
becomes, the more we try to reinsert tactility back into it.

However much electronic books may try to look like their
printed brethren, they still change how we manually interact with
them and those changes matter for how we read. There are, for

starters, no longer any pages to turn. There is no density to the e-book (all is battery), which is incidentally one of its greatest selling points. Open books can be measured by the sliding scale of pages past and future, like steps, just off to the side of the page. What lies *after* the digital page? An abyss. No matter what the page number says, we have no way to corroborate this evidence with our senses, no idea where we are while we read. The digital page isn't a window, it's a door (but like Bluebeard's castle: to where?). Perhaps Piranesi, with all of those stairwells that lead nowhere, should be considered the father of the digital page.

If we no longer turn the page, then what do we do? We have, at least for a little while longer, the button.[22] The hand no longer points, and thus cognitively and emotionally reaches for something it cannot have (like Michelangelo's famous finger), it *presses* or *squeezes*. The mechanical pressure that gave birth to the book in the form of the wooden handpress is today both vastly reduced in scale and multiplied in number through our interactions with the digital. There is a punctuatedness, a suddenness, but also a repetitiveness to pressing buttons that starkly contrast with the sedate rhythms of the slowly turned page. Buttons convert human motion into an electrical effect. In this, they preserve the idea of "conversion" that was at the core of reading books for Augustine. But in their incessant repetitiveness the meaning of conversion is gradually hollowed out, made less transformative. Conversion loses its singularity, as well as its totality. It is reduced to thousands of little turns. As Roland Barthes once remarked, "to repeat excessively is to enter into loss."[23]

But buttons also resist. Over time, their use causes stress to the human body, known as carpal tunnel syndrome. Like its related postural malady, "text neck," these syndromes are signs of how computation is beginning to stretch us, both cognitively and corporally.[24] The resistance of the button is an intimation of the way technology increasingly seems to be *pushing back*.

Perhaps it is for this reason that we are moving away from the world of the button to that of the touch screen. From the ugly three-dimensionality of the mechanical apparatus we ascend to the fantasy of existing in only two dimensions, a world of the single, yet infinite page. Here the finger no longer converts, but *conducts*. With capacitive touch screens your finger alters the screen's electrostatic field thereby conveying a command. Instead of pressing to turn the page, we now swipe and, at least for one reading interface, shake.[25] Kinesthesia, the sense of bodily movement, overrides the book's synesthesia, its unique art of conjoining touch, sight, and thought into a unified experience. In an electronic environment, corporal action overtakes reading's traditional inaction. Ever on the lookout for "impact" or "measurement" today, we appear to be increasingly afraid of reading's inertia.

The more my body does, however, the less my mind does. Interactivity is a constraint, not a freedom.[26] Swiping has the effect of making everything on the page cognitively lighter, less resistant. After all, the rhythmic swiping of the hand has been one of the most common methods of facilitating "speed-reading." And as one study after another affirms, the more time we spend reading screens, the less time we spend reading individual units of the text.[27] Skimming is the new normal. With my e-book, I no longer pause over the slight caress of the almost turned page—a rapture of anticipation—I just whisk away. Our hands become brooms, sweeping away the alphabetic dust before us.

In Judd Morrissey's *The Jew's Daughter* (2000), a title derived from a ballad sung in James Joyce's *Ulysses* and certainly one of the finest web fictions to date, we are presented with a single, yet unstable page (fig. 1.7).[28] As the cursor moves over highlighted words in the text, portions of the page suddenly change. It marks a nice inversion to Goldsmith's discretely revelatory cursor that brought text into view. In Morrissey we keep reading the same page over and over again, even as parts of it continue to change. We never "get" anywhere in this palimpsestual universe, just as it never stays the same.

The evanescence of *The Jew's Daughter* is everything that Anselm Kiefer's lead books were not. With even the barest proximity between the simulated forefinger and the simulated letter in

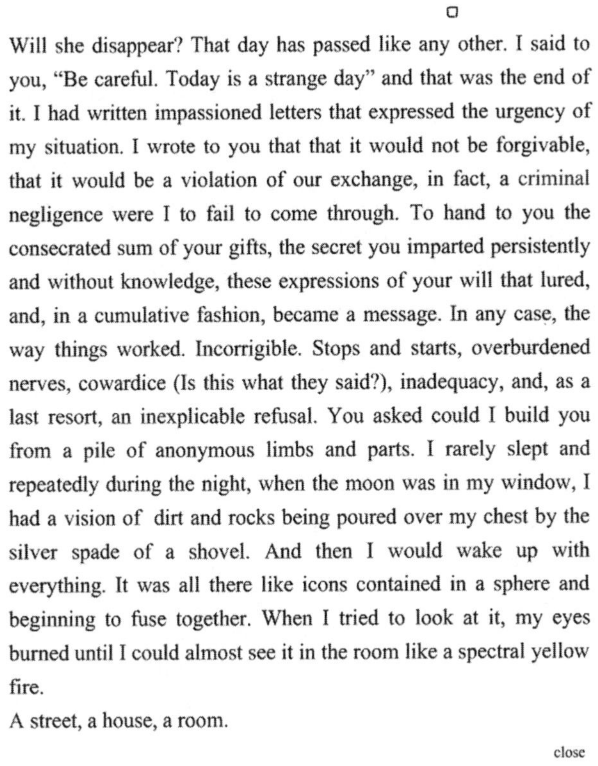

□

Will she disappear? That day has passed like any other. I said to you, "Be careful. Today is a strange day" and that was the end of it. I had written impassioned letters that expressed the urgency of my situation. I wrote to you that that it would not be forgivable, that it would be a violation of our exchange, in fact, a criminal negligence were I to fail to come through. To hand to you the consecrated sum of your gifts, the secret you imparted persistently and without knowledge, these expressions of your will that lured, and, in a cumulative fashion, became a message. In any case, the way things worked. Incorrigible. Stops and starts, overburdened nerves, cowardice (Is this what they said?), inadequacy, and, as a last resort, an inexplicable refusal. You asked could I build you from a pile of anonymous limbs and parts. I rarely slept and repeatedly during the night, when the moon was in my window, I had a vision of dirt and rocks being poured over my chest by the silver spade of a shovel. And then I would wake up with everything. It was all there like icons contained in a sphere and beginning to fuse together. When I tried to look at it, my eyes burned until I could almost see it in the room like a spectral yellow fire.

A street, a house, a room.

close

[FIGURE 1.7] The first "page" from Judd Morrissey, *The Jew's Daughter* (2000). The lines beginning with the words "and without knowledge" and ending with the words "in my window, I" will disappear and be replaced by new lines when the cursor touches the highlighted word "criminal." Reproduced courtesy of the artist.

Morrissey, text can suddenly not be there. It replaces the durable impression of the printing press or the less durable pressure of the button with the instability of electronic projection. When we touch texts in an online world, Morrissey reminds us, they can change in an instant. My hold over them is less secure. Contact is now conductivity.

As the digital scholar Matthew Kirschenbaum has recently cautioned us, however, digital texts are both notoriously difficult to preserve and *incredibly hard to delete*.[29] Reading my old Apple IIe diskettes today is as difficult as trying to completely erase my current hard drive (the National Security Administration recommends that anything short of immolation is not entirely foolproof). Digital texts are both sticky and fragile, hard to hold on to and hard to let go of.[30]

Kirschenbaum's reminder is a timely one, a welcome correction to the widespread belief in the instability of digital texts. But what strikes me as even more important is not this apparent choice between preservation and loss, between claims of one medium being more or less stable than another. Rather, at issue is understanding the way these two categories, the lost and found, mutually inform one another as conditions of knowledge. In the nineteenth century, it had become fashionable to travel to old libraries and scour collections for "lost" manuscripts, ultimately with the aim of publishing them in print, much like the itinerant humanists of the sixteenth and seventeenth centuries had done before them. The losability (and thus discoverability) of manuscript sources had become a key complement to reading printed books. The sense of print's durability depended upon an imagined sense of the perishability of handwriting, although this was by no means actually the case (compare the longevity of many medieval manuscripts with the fragility of Renaissance chapbooks or much nineteenth-century ephemera and you will see what I mean). Printed books, too, can come and go. Indeed, the more there were of them the more they required vigilant attention to ensure their proper reproduction over time. The sense of lost-and-foundness that belonged to reading in the nineteenth century was an essential component of the rising historical awareness that gripped the century and that is in many ways still with us. Thinking historically rests on the contradictory notion of something being both simultaneously present and absent, on grasping and letting go.

Scholars of the future will no doubt troll libraries to locate "lost" print editions of undigitized texts, just like their print predecessors scoured libraries for lost manuscripts. At the same time, like their print predecessors, they will also work tirelessly on preserving digital texts through time, maintaining our hold over the written record, as the great British editor Richard Bentley had done in the eighteenth century and as Kirschenbaum and others are beginning to do today.[31] But what matters to such future endeavors is not some ultimate hoped for completion of the digital record—that we will digitize all the books (or all the pieces of paper in the world) or that all digital texts will be preserved forever. Rather, these archival practices are important because they engage in the oscillatory rhythms of the lost and found of historical thinking, something that was itself very much a product of modern bookish learning. By drawing attention to the incomplete remnants of print or the challenging legacies of the digital, scholars can help complicate beliefs about digital writing as something either purely evanescent or permanently present, what Kirschenbaum calls "the long now" of software. They will lend digital writing a sense of temporary closure, a sense of internal differentiation with itself.

Perhaps this is what is ultimately most interesting about Morrissey's digital page in *The Jew's Daughter*—the way its instability is compensated for by the imposed act of rereading. It keeps repeating itself with a difference. Only *portions* of the text fly away and are replaced when we touch them. Morrissey's single page has the structure of a refrain about it, like the genre of the ballad from which it derives its inspiration. As a work, it mixes novelty and repetition, instability with iterability, which has been at the heart of all true knowledge regardless of the medium. Plato famously said that the problem of writing is that it keeps telling us the same thing over and over again.[32] Morrissey's digital answer is, sort of. There is a great deal of wisdom preserved in this "sort of," in reading's dialectic of the lost and found.

+ +

Tonight I will read to my children before they go to bed. Although the "bedtime story" was only invented as a common practice at the end of the nineteenth century, there has always been a durable physiological connection between sleep and reading.[33] Unlike the nursemaid's oral tales that were meant to frighten children into staying in their beds (magnificently parodied by the fantasist E. T. A. Hoffmann in *The Sandman*), the slightly monotonous rhythm of parents' reading aloud is imagined to be a more effective way of accessing the unconsciousness of sleep.

Once the circus of getting ready for bed is over (why pajamas are so hard to put on is a mystery), we search out a clear plot of carpet and choose a book to read. Maybe it will be something from the Frog and Toad series or Tinker and Tanker or, the house favorite, George and Martha. The prevalence of so many pairs reminds me that children's books are often concerned with the ambiguous sociability of reading, the way we are both together and apart when we read. In this, these books nicely recall that first great childish reader, Don Quixote, and his pint-sized literary companion.

As I begin to read, the kids begin to lean into me. Our bodies assume positions of rest, the book our shared column of support. No matter what advertisers say, this could never be true of the acrobatic screen. As we gradually sink into the floor, and each other, our minds are freed to follow their own pathways, unlike the prescribed pathways of the web. We read and we drift. "The words of my book nothing," writes Walt Whitman, "the drift of it everything."[34]

New research continues to emphasize the importance of mind wandering for learning.[35] It turns out that *not* paying attention is one of the best ways of discovering new ideas. Reading books, whether silently or aloud, remains one of the most efficient means of enabling such errant thinking. As our bodies rest, our minds begin to work in a different way. New connections, new pathways, and sharp turns are being made as we meander our way through the book, but also away from it. There is no way to tell if anyone is actually paying attention anymore as I read, including myself. This seems to be one of the great benefits of reading aloud, that you can think of something else while you do it. We may be holding the book together, but our minds are no doubt far apart by now. The fairy tale is the first story of childhood because it tells of such leaving behind (parents and home), of entering the dreamscape of the woods—and the mind. It tells of the crooked path of change. How can one know where reading books ends and dreaming in books begins?

We come back in the end to Dr. Faustus, who was one of the most important folk heroes of the world of printed books and a rough contemporary of Don Quixote. Faust was a product of early modern learning, of all those books that were increasingly available to readers. Faust was Quixote's serious side. Unlike the Don, however, who steadily devoured works of fiction, Faust tried to know too much about the world. He tried to surpass what could be known in a book, whether it was the Bible or the alchemical handbook. Faust, the fist, in other words, is our modern day demon, not Mephistopheles, his devilish double. Faust reminds us of the way books are totems against ceaseless activity, tools for securing the somatic calm that is the beginning of all careful but also visionary thought. If we believe in the value of rest, and the kind of conversional thinking that it makes possible, then we will want to preserve books and their spaces of readerly rest.

But Faust also reminds us not to hold on too tightly. He shows us the risks of grasping. I find joy in the way words escape me with Morrissey, in their lightness, the way I can make them go away. They remind me that the meaning of reading lies in the oscillatory rhythms of the opening and closing hand.

TWO

Face, Book

As for me, I came expecting to see faces and see nothing but backs!

VICTOR HUGO [*notre dame de paris*]

Beneath the lines of every book is a face. This is the lesson of Honoré de Balzac's masterpiece *The Unknown Masterpiece* (1832–45), the story of the young seventeenth-century artist Nicolas Poussin, who gains entry into the studio of the age's most famous (and fictional) painter, Master Frenhofer. Frenhofer will finally reveal his life's masterpiece, a portrait of a young woman. Poussin and his guide, François Porbus, move themselves expectantly in front of the painting. They are shocked at what they see, or rather, don't see: there is no portrait, just a mass of wavy lines (and one beautiful foot).

"Do you see anything?" Poussin asked of Porbus.
"No...do you?"
"I see nothing."

The two young men strain to see through the lines, "moving first to the right, then to the left, then head-on (*de face*), lowering and raising themselves by turns." Finally, after glimpsing the foot, Porbus exclaims, "There is a woman beneath!" The narrator continues, "Both artists turned involuntarily to Frenhofer. They began to have some understanding, vague though it was, of the ecstasy in which he lived."[1] The next day when Porbus returns he learns that Frenhofer has burned his work and died in the night.

In his fiction about the face composed of wavy lines, Balzac was asking what it is we see when we read a book. Books have never just been objects of reading. To understand books is to understand the act of looking that transpires between us and them.[2] It is to ask how we face books and how they face us.

Faces abound in books, no more so than in the emerging vogue of the authorial frontispiece that set in at the turn of the seventeenth century, the age of Poussin, Rembrandt, and Caravaggio and the first golden age of print, of *Don Quixote*, Shakespeare's first folio, and Racine's *Oeuvres* (of which twenty different editions were published by the end of the century).[3] For Balzac, who was writing for an era that saw the vast commodification of the authorial portrait (Byron was its muse), not everyone could see the face *behind* the book, the human dimension that coursed like tendrils through the work and that was not just slapped on its surface.[4] It took a particular kind of looking to see this face, not just the visionary kind that might not be there, like Frenhofer, when you woke up in the morning. One only saw this face if one looked "by turns." Head-on (*de face*), Balzac wants us to know, we will never see the true face of the book. It is no accident that Picasso, the great cubist, created an exquisite illustrated edition of Balzac's tale (fig. 2.1).

Today, the Web is awash with faces. We are all Byron now. As one commentator remarked, "We've turned the web into a vast narcissistic culture."[5] The face continues to serve as one of the most common techniques for organizing our interactions with new media (not for nothing do we speak of interfaces). Faces are how we make sense of technologies and ourselves through them. Facebook isn't a quaint gesture of remediation. It is an urgent, massive cultural attempt to understand.

As faces consume more and more of what and how we read, it is worth asking how the history of reading has been bound up with the history of looking, and looking at faces in particular. Faces are forms of intimacy. They are where we learn to identify,

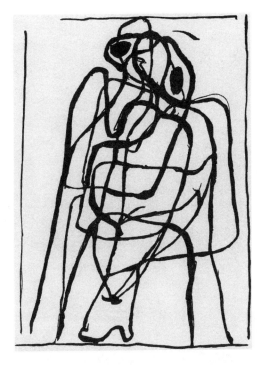

[FIGURE 2.1]   Honoré de Balzac, *Le Chef-d'oeuvre inconnu.*
Eaux-fortes originales et dessins gravés sur bois de Pablo
Picasso (1931), 80. © Picasso Estate/SODRAC (2011).

and identify with, things. What can the history of the book's many faces tell us about the future of reading?

+ +

One of the earliest authorial frontispieces in a printed book is not insignificantly from a translation: John Harington's translation of Ludovico Ariosto's *Orlando Furioso* (1591) (fig. 2.2). Here we see Harington in the bottom portion of the engraving, kept company by his faithful dog as a reminder to readers of his own fidelity as a translator ("traduttore, traditore," as the Italians

[FIGURE 2.2] Frontispiece from John Harington's
translation of *Orlando Furioso* (1591). By permission of the
Master and Fellows of St. John's College, Cambridge.

have it, every translation betrays its original). Up above there is
a bust of Ariosto, a modern classic, as the two writers, set amid a
larger architectural edifice, mark out the North and South Poles
of European literature.

"Frontispiece" has come to mean any illustration facing the
title page, but initially it meant to look at head-on: *frontispicium*,
from *frons* (forehead) and *specio* (to look). In its earliest form it

applied to architecture, meaning a "facade." As sixteenth-century writers like Harington were well aware, it was Pindar who first equated writing with building (as in his sixth Olympic ode: "As when we contrive a stately mansion, supporting on golden pillars the well-built portal of the edifice, we will construct the hymn").[6] The frontispiece, pioneered in woodcuts by artists like Lucas Cranach the Elder in Wittenberg in the early sixteenth century, was both an edifice and a portal. It gave the book definition, and it provided an opening. It was another indication of the way rest, as in resting on (like all those columns that adorned early modern frontispieces), was the precondition of bookish thought. Books support our turn inward.

Like books and buildings, letters, too, have many faces. Whether it is the notion of "typeface" or the practice of illuminating letters with faces in manuscripts and early printed books (fig. 2.3), the faces of the letter are numerous. In some cases, as in Antonio Basoli's *Alfabeto Pittorico* (1839) or Johann David Steingruber's *Architectonisches Alphabeth* (1773), the faces of buildings were imagined to be in the shape of letters. Books, buildings, and letters all converge around the figure of the face.

The frontispiece to Harington's translation is accordingly covered in faces (twenty-eight as far as I can tell), including the two "authors" on the title page. Where the translator looks back at us, the poet Ariosto looks away. We only see half of his face, and his poetry. But which half comes through in translation? Reading as a form of turning in, the frontispiece tells us, is also a form of turning away—from the world, but also from the text, which is never wholly our own. Like those monstrous faces that grow out of the architectural facade or all those Italian *o*'s that turn into Anglo-Saxon consonants (more monsters), we turn away in order to transform. The face not only faces us, it also marks a turning point. The face is a space of translation.

The frontispieces of books are a reminder of the way reading is at bottom always multiple. Reading involves an act of translation between itself and the act of looking. As recent research in

[FIGURE 2.3] In this decorated letter *N*, we see an image of
Louis IX holding a miniature of Saint Chapelle, the beautiful chapel
he commissioned to be built in the heart of Paris in 1248.
The image conjoins letter, face, and architectural facade
all within a single frame. Cholet Master, *Grandes chroniques
de France* (1275/1310), BSG MS 782 fol. 327. Photo
IRHT © Bibliothèque Sainte-Geneviève, Paris.

neuroscience suggests, we see letters in much the same way as we
perceive everyday objects through a process of combining more
elementary shapes. The faces of letters are composed of geometric
patterns already found in nature, "topological invariants" in the
words of the neuroscientists.[7] Or you could say we see objects in
the same way as we read letters. There is a deep-rooted connec-

tion between legibility and visuality. The face is where reading and seeing merge. We see letters, and we read faces.

Perhaps the best example of this idea comes from one of the most famous books of faces, Johann Lavater's four-volume *Physiognomic Fragments* (1775), which contains over eight hundred illustrations of faces. The Swiss pastor believed you could divine a person's soul from his or her face and that such divination would one day be quantifiable as a science (not for nothing was the Age of Enlightenment also known as the Age of Quackery). Lavater's work became a European sensation, translated into seven languages by the end of the century, and emerged as one of the most important, if also troubling, landmarks to the face of the book (it later gave birth to the field of phrenology and its use by the Nazis in the twentieth century).[8]

To his contemporaries, however, Lavater's book helped set in motion the silhouette craze of the late eighteenth century, named after Etienne de Silhouette, who had a fondness for cutout images of acquaintances' profiles. Lavater taught readers to find meaning in the outlines of the human face, but also how to read shadows (fig. 2.4). "A person's silhouette is the weakest, the emptiest and at the same time the truest and most faithful image that one can make of a person," he wrote in his characteristic sentimental style.[9]

For Lavater and his contemporaries, the book of silhouettes was an important visual tool. In learning how to read the contrasts between the black-and-white contours of the face, readers were learning how to see the world as one vast legible page.[10] It was a telling sign of the way reading in the eighteenth century was gradually colonizing the world of looking (though we may worry about its opposite today). "Listen," says Faust in Paul Valéry's *Mon Faust*, a twentieth-century rewriting of the myth, "I want to create a great work, a book…" To which Mephisto replies, "You? Aren't you satisfied with being a book?"[11] From the eighteenth century onward, wherever people looked they saw (through) their books.

As our world becomes more intensely visual by the day, we

[FIGURE 2.4] "An ordinary Physionomist will pronounce of what that head is capable or incapable, as soon as he has seen the very remarkable section of the profile which is between *a* and *b*; a good Observer will decide it by that which is between *e* and *d*; and finally, the real Connoisseur will need no more, to settle his judgement, than the space between *a* and *e*." Image of Abbé Raynal in Johann Caspar Lavater, *Essays on Physiognomy, Designed to Promote the Knowledge and the Love of Mankind*, vol. 1 (1789), 251. Courtesy of the Osler Library of the History of Medicine, McGill University, Montreal, Quebec, Canada.

often forget the important role that books have played in shaping our perception. Books change how we look, not just in the sense of how we see but also how we are seen. This point was beautifully explored in the work of the Victorian photographer Julia Margaret Cameron (1815–79), who was born in Calcutta and lived for many years as a neighbor to Alfred Lord Tennyson on the Isle of Wight. Cameron worked in a century overwhelmed by books, but also by photography—by the 1860s, 300–400 *million* miniature photographic portraits printed on *cartes de visite* were being sold in London every year. As historians of photography have recently begun to remind us, the birth of photography was intimately related to the history of the book.[12] For Cameron, who liked to collect her portraits into albums, there was something decidedly bookish about the way she understood the new visual art. As she wrote to the natural scientist John Herschel, who introduced her to photography, "Yes—the history of the human face is a book we don't tire of if we can get its grand truths and learn them by heart."[13]

Cameron's photographs are suffused with a strong sense of the turning that belonged to reading books. Perhaps it was due to the fact that prior to becoming a photographer she was a translator of the most famous illustrated ballad to come out of the eighteenth century, Gottfried August Bürger's *Leonora*. For Cameron, the spirit of photography was born out of the transformative practices of translation.[14] When we look at the portraits of her sitters, particularly her female sitters, we see how one of their most pronounced features is the way they turn, sometimes wistfully, sometimes aggressively, away from us. Whether it is the strained neck muscles in the portrait of her niece, *Julia Jackson* (1867), the future mother of Virginia Woolf; the signature botanical swirl in the unforgettable rosebush of *The Gardener's Daughter* (1867); or her telltale soft focus, as in *The Dream* (1869) (fig. 2.5), Cameron's women are decidedly vorticular.

The veiled young woman of *The Dream* is one of many of Cameron's women who take flight, like the children she liked to photograph while sleeping or dressed as angels. In the foreground we see how the woman's long hair is blurred, an undulating screen that keeps us slightly at bay. Only in the background, in the picture's depth, does she come into focus. As she recedes, she is held back by an ambiguous hand that reaches for her broach, a subtle play on the pull of portraiture, which derives from the Latin *traho*, "to draw in." The broach, the very center of the

[FIGURE 2.5]   Julia Margaret Cameron, *The Dream*
(1869). Courtesy of the National Media Museum/
Science and Society Picture Library, UK.

portrait, is also a clasp, that which binds her shroud around her and one of the most important icons in the history of books. In the play of grasping and retreating that marks out Cameron's image, the photographic portrait mirrors the medium of the book in which it will eventually appear and to which it pays a kind of *homage*. Cameron's crowning project would be an illustrated edition of Tennyson's *Idylls of the King*, where the photographic portrait is imagined as reading's double.

If, for artists like Balzac and Cameron, beneath the lines of every book is a face, what then is beneath the face? In *Facile* (1935), a collaboration between the poet Paul Eluard and the photographer Man Ray, we are offered a tentative answer. In one poem, the face of a young woman has been cut off by the edge of the page. For the surrealist Man Ray, behind the human face is just another face, this time of the page. In books, it seems, we never get past the face. In Rainer Maria Rilke's modernist novel of a psychologically unstable young man in Paris, *The Notebooks of Malte Laurids Brigge* (1910), we are told the story of a woman who left her face in her hands one day when she looked up. It is an unbearable sight, like looking at angels. We cannot bear, so Rilke tells us, to see behind the face.

This, then, is the paradoxical end of reading as looking: no matter how often we turn the face of the page, we never get anything more than the face—of yet another page. There is a repetitiveness to the look of reading, one that propels the readers' quest for something more, a desire to look through, past, or beyond. Perhaps the history of reading addiction—that all too common desire to finish all of the books—can be understood as the hope to find more than a face when we read, to finally find a body or a *corpus*. As Eudora Welty remarked about when she was a child, "I looked for the book I couldn't have and it was a row. That was how I learned about the Series Books. There were many of everything, generations of everybody, instead of one. I wasn't coming to the end of reading, after all—I was saved."[15] The faces of the book go on and on. Reading's salvation is also reading's curse. Cameron knew this; she inscribed lines from Milton's sonnet "On his deceased wife" onto a copy of *The Dream* that she included in an album to a friend:

> Her face was vail'd, yet to my fancied sight,
> Love, sweetness, goodness, in her person shin'd
> So clear, as in no face with more delight.
> But O as to embrace me she enclin'd
> I wak'd, she fled, and day brought back my night.

The bookish face ultimately marks a line of flight. Every frontispiece is a death mask.

+ +

The online face, by contrast, is always too close. I am curiously drawn to the uncomfortable crampedness of the face of the webcam.[16] It marks a distinct inversion of Cameron's Victorian vision of receding women. Instead of the book's impressions, the webcam captures a sense of compression as one of the essential features of the digital. For Walter Benjamin, German-Jewish philosopher and one of the twentieth-century's great theorists of new media, photographic portraits from the nineteenth century revealed entire, and entirely lost, worlds that unfolded out of the photograph's plane.[17] According to Benjamin, the look of the nineteenth-century face expressed a sense of lost time, famously captured in the stern, yet longing eyes of the philosopher Friedrich Schelling. In today's webcam portraits, by contrast, time looks crowded, heavy, *compressed*.

"I have no idea what time it is," begins Ellen Ullman's cult memoir of being a software engineer in *Close to the Machine* (1997). It is the pitch-perfect reversal of Proust's opening gambit from *In Search of Lost Time* that begins, "For a long time..." The closeness of the screen unsettles, it infiltrates our sense of temporal sequence. "I have passed through a membrane where the real world and its uses no longer matter," continues Ullman. "I am a software engineer."[18] The idea of "lost time" takes on a whole new meaning online—not in the sense of an irrevocable pastness, a nostalgia; instead, time itself is now what is lost. We are losing our sense of time online.

In new media parlance, this means that we are now "always on."[19] Fatigue is one of the basic conditions of the digital. When we look at screens we become prematurely tired, the optical equivalent of carpal tunnel syndrome. In this, digital reading marks a return to what it must have been like to read by candlelight, only now there is too much backlighting, or too little up front, as in the undifferentiated grayscape of electronic ink. But we are also tired because of the permanent arousal that screens promise. We know about the history of pornographic books (there were many), but books either were or were not erotic.[20] Digital interfaces, by contrast, always *might be*. With its endlessly rotating panoply of masturbating men, Chatroulette.com might just be the perfect crystallization of the web's visual nature.[21]

For Benjamin, the punctuated stimulations of new visual media like photography or the cinema offered a sense of what he optimistically called "awakening."[22] There was a messianic sense about them that seems almost impossible to embrace today. One century later, we might say that instead of awakening our relationship to the incessant on-ness of the digital could be categorized as a form of sleepwalking, an idea coined by Benjamin's contemporary, the novelist Hermann Broch, in his modernist landmark *The Sleepwalkers* (1932). We may dream in books, or awake in the cinema, but we sleepwalk through the web.

By this I do not mean to suggest that we are more thoughtless online (the cliché of becoming shallower). Sleepwalking is different than dreaming because it marks out a confusion of categories. When we dream we are still asleep. When we sleepwalk, by contrast, we are mentally asleep, and yet physically awake. We are out of sync with our ourselves and our world. Sleepwalking represents a clash of states. "Underneath the visible soporific nature of life lay a constant tension of the individual elements," writes Broch of his heroine, Hanna Wendling. "Were you to excise a single piece from the fabric of her reality, you would find a monstrous torsion, a paroxysm of molecules."[23] If the bookish world of frontispieces was a world of death masks—of flights from reality—the world of digital faces is full of such "monstrous torsions," paroxysms of multiple states of being (tired, virtual, real, simulated, artificial, bored, enhanced, transformed, etc.). The digital portrait is a persistent encounter with the face of the not exactly vital. The 419 letter, the sock puppet, the printable organ, or even searingly banal web pages like "That Was NOT Your Last Piece of Gum Stop Lying" (3,015,023 likes on Facebook at last count) are the novel faces of text today. The zombie is our new *Doppelgänger*. As Brian Christian writes, reading has become a permanent Turing test to assess where the machine ends and the human begins.[24]

No other website has modeled our encounter with screens on the face more thoroughly of course than Facebook. Facebook is the almost perfect rejection of Balzac's prohibition of the "head-on" or *de face*. Facebook is so many faces, insistent, protruding, in *your* face. But on the other hand, Facebook is pure profile (your user "profile" being the core of social networking). However unconsciously, it counts Lavater as one of its forefathers.

And yet unlike the boundedness of the silhouette, the essence of the Facebook profile is that I am always more than myself, what one commentator has cleverly called the new "narcisystem."[25] In place of the many angles of the bookish face—the condition of its ineffability—the new online face is composed of numerous *other* people's faces. It is a return to the idea of preformationism, that all beings are contained in every single being in a kind of universal *potentia*. There is something deeply theological, but also grotesque, about this idea of the personal assemblage, nicely captured in Daniel Gordon's celebrated portraits that are collages of images found online (fig. 2.6).

For generations of artists and writers, envisioning with books began with a sense of looking away. In a world of social networking this turns instead into an act of "looking on"—looking on others in a kind of permanent state of voyeurism and looking onto the next person in a great chain (or collage) of being. Unlike the black box of the bibliographic silhouette, the digital profile is the sum of other egos. From the Freudian (and decidedly bookish) notion of the "ego" with its quaint tripartite structure (ego, id, and superego), we should now more properly be speaking of the digital *egology*, the ecological ego. Beneath the bookish face was nothing but an unsettling void. Beneath the digital face lies instead the graph, the new optical unconscious.[26] Balzac's unknown masterpiece—that haze of wavy lines that covered over

[FIGURE 2.6]   Daniel Gordon, *Red Headed Woman* (2008).
Gordon's work has shown in the Museum of Modern Art in
New York, and he is considered one of the most innovative
new portraitists today. Image courtesy of the artist.

the face—has been turned inside out. Instead of the face being
beneath the text, underneath the face of digital text is always
more text (first graph, then code). A host of new media projects,
such as Giselle Beiguelman's *Code UP* (2004), Lisa Jevbratt's
1:1 (1999), or Ryoji Ikeda's *Datamatics* (2006), are attempts to
visualize the text beneath the image, to see the conditions of how
we look digitally.

Few issues surround Facebook, or digital media more generally, more ominously than that of surveillance.[27] Facebook's
corporate success is largely related to the way it has been able

to monetize *oversight*. "Access," one of the great rallying cries of new media throughout the ages, no longer only implies access to something, but also access to someone. From the early dreams of digital texts as the offspring of Proteus, an endless transformability, we have awoken to find a retail panopticon where everything we say or see is observed, counted, and recorded. Not just speech, but the "page view" is the new ore. In the nineteenth century, the "view" stood for a popular genre of illustrated books, consisting of picturesque tours of ruins, cathedrals, bowers, gardens, and distant, hazy horizons. The bookish view stood for a suite of visual and emotional vanishing points. Today, the "view" implies that *you* are being looked at. Instead of the book as window—of seeing through books—social networking is a metalabyrinth of mutual regard. Even readerly underlining, once the bastion of self-referentiality, is now being viewed for marketing purposes with the help of electronic readers. There is no outside the network today except the ever dwindling space-time of off. As Don DeLillo writes in *Valparaiso*, his satirical drama of contemporary media, "Everything is the interview."[28] We have returned to a world before the invention of privacy.

Ironically, the blurred face has returned as a compelling new symbol of this digital condition. For Cameron, the blur stood for a sense of an individual's ineffability, what we could not know. The digital blur, by contrast, is a sign of the breakdown of mutuality, of someone knowing too much. In Michael Wolf's recent prize-winning exhibit *I See You* (2010), drawn from images from Google Street View, or Manu Luksch's *Faceless* (2007), a video drawn from closed-circuit television in London in which other people's faces had to be legally blurred when she requested access to them (fig. 2.7), the blur is central to the meaning of the digital portrait.[29] These works ask us what it means to be seen, or to have one's seeing seen, without one's knowledge, to be captured without consent. The blur is not a sign of some ethical response—here, I've blurred your face, now it's OK. For these artists, the blur is a sign of something that cannot entirely be undone, that

[FIGURE 2.7]   Video still from Manu Luksch,
Faceless (2007). In the video, Luksch tells the story of a
woman in search of a face. Courtesy of the artist.

cannot entirely be *effaced*. It cannot be undone, but it also cannot
be condoned. The blurred face of Google Street View or closed-
circuit television is a sign of an ethical breakdown in the new
system of digital looking.

+ +

The first faces most of us encounter in books are those of animals. The animal face, so central to the children's tale, does many
things: it reminds us of our place in the natural world; it helps
us confront our fears (animals in books can be cuddly, but also
ambiguously fanged); but most of all animal faces are thought
to be simple.[30] They can stand for something in the way that hu-

man faces cannot. The symbolic simplicity of the animal's face is a very good way of learning not only how to read faces, but how to read.

When my children no longer want me to read books to them at night they will no doubt move on to social networking software. They will transition from learning to understand the faces of animals to those of their teenage peers (a remarkable continuity you might say). The looking through and looking away of the book (what did Mole, Rat, and Badger really mean?) will turn to the looking on of the networked profile. How will they learn to negotiate the mobility of online friendship versus the static nature of making friends with the people of their books? How will they deal with the challenges of the asynchronous viewing that belongs to social networking (I don't see that you see me) versus the one-way viewing of the printed book?

The answer that I have to offer is not uncharacteristically anachronistic. It is to return to a different time and place: the novel of the baroque court (I can hear the sighing now). Madeleine de Scudéry, María de Zayas, Madame de Lafayette—these are the great theorists of public performance and the travails of personal privacy. As women they were acutely aware of the limited spaces of personal aloneness; as members of court they were attuned to the seething judgments of interlocking social circles; and as writers they knew firsthand of the incalculable responses of a newly burgeoning literary market. These books show us how unnerving it is to suddenly hear your own story told back to you (*La Princesse de Clèves*) or how serious the moral consequences are of betraying someone else's story (*Novelas amorosas y ejemplares*). They teach us what it is like to live in a world of always being seen, but also to learn to take care of narratives entrusted to us.

We often hear that there is too much confession today, and by association too much voyeurism. We are haunted by the ghost of Rousseau, whose *Confessions* (1782) changed the reading world for good. I suspect that this is nothing more than a veiled elitism, a feeling shared among many that not everyone should be able to represent his or herself, a sentiment echoed through the ages. I personally cannot help thinking that social media will make us more, not less, receptive to friendship, just as eighteenth-century Pietists imagined we became more receptive to God by reflecting on ourselves everyday with pen and paper. Writing about oneself and photographing oneself doesn't have to be seen as the consummate act of narcissism that it is often portrayed to be. It can also be a way of opening ourselves up to others. But social media can also teach us to have a sense of playfulness about our identities, like Henri Beyle, aka Stendhal, that great Romantic epigone of the baroque who employed close to two hundred and fifty pseudonyms throughout his life. Like Beyle, I want my kids to learn the art of pseudonymity in a world that has largely given up on anonymity. In response to the privatization of the public sphere, we need a renewed sense of public dissimulation.

Mostly, though, I hope that as my children learn more about these bygone worlds and their halls of mirrors they will learn to relate to others without fully needing to know them, to be able to turn off their looking glasses. I want them to value the recognition of another's privacy, the night of knowledge in the words of Milton's prophetic sonnet. Or as Rilke wrote to his friend, the artist Paula Modersohn-Becker, "I consider this to be the highest task of the union of two people: that each one should keep watch over the solitude of the other."[31]

Reading books, and looking on the world through books, teaches us to relate to that which we cannot fully know. Books teach us to see the world multiply, from all its angles. The multiple faces of books presuppose a nonknowledge of another that has deep ethical implications ("I wak'd, she fled," as Milton writes). The digital face, on the other hand, encourages us to see the world *as* multiple, as consisting of hybrids, compositions, or "paroxysms," in Hermann Broch's words. Facebook presupposes an inherent presence of another, that there is no I without You, and that, too, is ethically profound. There is an entanglement to social networking that is as meaningful as the book's pedagogy of mental distance, that I can never in the end fully know you.

As the eighteenth-century Swiss pastor Johann Lavater understood, reading faces is an essential human task. It forms the basis of the act of "acknowledgment" that is the prerequisite of all political, social, and moral equality.[32] The face is where we recognize each other in a social sense. Learning how to read faces—how to master the double act of looking and reading, whether online or off—is where we learn to care about something and someone without a sense of possession. If holding is a precondition of dreaming, facing is a precondition of caring. It is through faces where we meet others at a distance. We embrace another with our hands, but we greet others at a distance with our faces. The face is where we learn to be together apart. If we value this apartness as much as we value being social, then we will need to hold on to books and their faces. Unlike social networking, in books no one is looking where you are looking.

THREE

Turning the Page
(Roaming, Zooming, Streaming)

Pages so many, paper so much!
WALTER SCOTT [*waverley*]

All is leaf!
J. W. GOETHE

The page is the atom of the book, its most basic building block (and like atoms it too consists of smaller elements, soot, gum, hide, linen, pulp, thread, so many bibliographic quarks). But the page is also a frame, that which marks a boundary. For almost two millennia the page has been the primary way that we have accessed reading. The page is where words assume order, and it is that order that has helped shape the meaning of words for us.

Until now, digital texts have largely not departed from the page view (even if, in an interesting case of double remediation they have incorporated the logic of the scroll into the page). Websites are stacked piles of pages, browsers are static "windows," and e-books aren't simulations of books at all, but single pages. In Goethe's words, all is still very much leaf or page. Or better yet: today, all is recto.

Much of the current debate about the future of reading turns on the *crowdedness* of the digital page versus its bookish predecessor. There is just too much stuff on the screen now. The web-cam portrait is the new face of text. We are breeding generations of distracted readers, people who simply cannot pay attention long enough to finish a book.

This is undoubtedly true, but only to a point. We have of course been here before. "Read much, not many," said Pliny the Younger in the first century AD, initiating a standard refrain about reading through the ages.[1] We have always worried about how to instill careful reading, no matter what the object. Keats said to read one page of poetry per day.[2] Erasmus suggested to read the Gospels by "bit[ing] off some of this medicine constantly...chew it assiduously and pass it down into our spiritual stomachs [and] do not cast it up again."[3] Alongside the slow food movement we now have (once again) appeals for slow reading (and of course antiregurgitation).[4]

But we have also been here before in terms of page design. The medieval page reveled in its cacophony (fig. 3.1). So did the great printed critical editions of the sixteenth- and seventeenth-century humanists, like Joseph Scaliger or Daniel Heinsius.[5] As much as I like the geometric asceticism that printed pages can take (from early sixteenth-century Aldine editions to Romantic promoters of the wide margins in the nineteenth century), I am also drawn to the full page of the book. The scribal and scholarly commitment to textual abundance suggests an exuberance about reading that I hope we will never forget. Our notebooks still often look like this. They are reminders of the spillage of human thought.

Of course there is something markedly different about the digital page. Medieval or Renaissance marginalia don't blink. (Is there anything more offensive to the eye than blinking lights, which have always been meant as warning signals?) If e-books today are serene imitators of the modern printed page, "enhanced" e-books, every publisher's dream, will soon consist of vast amounts of animation (sound tracks, pop-up windows, and moving images). If I were designing a reader today in our age of enhancement, I would call it The Pygmalion.

It may be that we should no longer even call this reading.

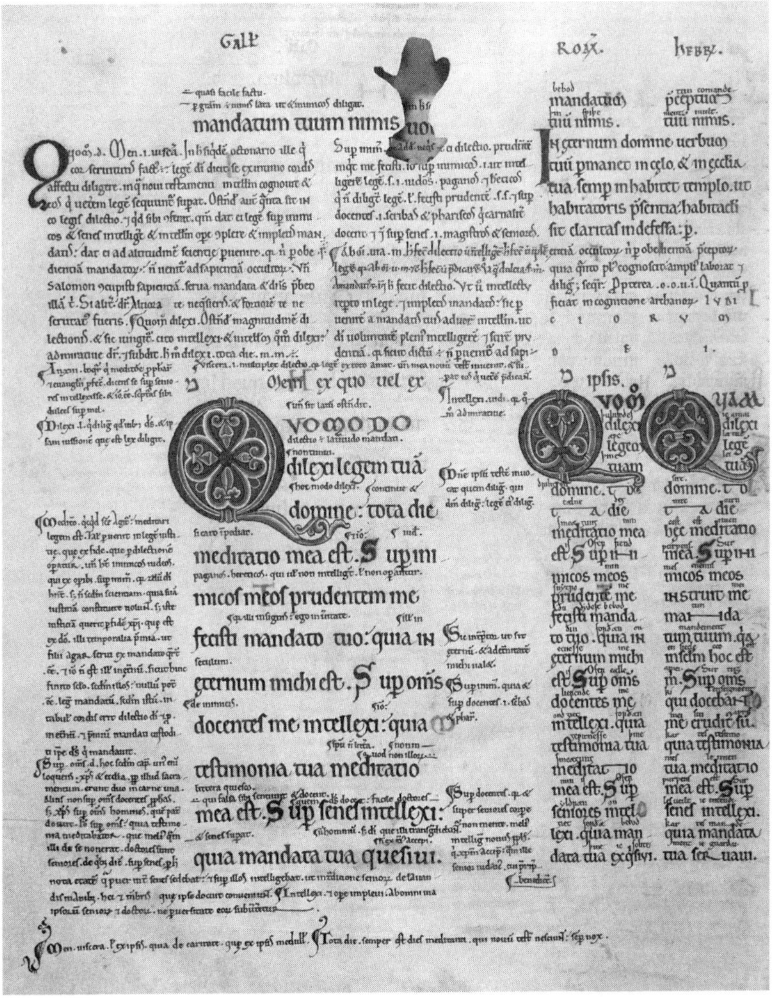

[FIGURE 3.1]   Three versions of Psalm 118 based on St. Jerome's edition. The left column is the Gallican text with Latin interlinear gloss from the church fathers. The middle column is the Roman text with an Anglo-Saxon interlinear translation. And the right column is the Hebrew text with French interlinear translation. From *The Canterbury Psalter* (1147), MS R.17.1 fol. 219v. By permission of the Master and Fellows of Trinity College, Cambridge.

Listening to music, watching movies, pointing, and clicking—these have nothing to do with reading. But we should also remember that reading has very often had this "multimedial" quality about it, even if not in such an overpopulated sense. Reading has traditionally been imbedded in aural practices of reading aloud (whether in school, church, at the dinner table, before bed, or for the visually impaired), just as, as I tried to show in the last chapter, it has so often been codefined by the act of looking (ceremonial books, travel books, and coffee-table books to name a few). In my own house as a child, reading was definitely loud. Family members were constantly reading their favorite passages aloud or shouting, "Look at this!" (like a parental pop-up window). Digital texts may be different in degree—in the way they are able to amplify our historical relations to the page (more crowded, more multimedial)—but they are not truly different in kind. They still do not, as yet, depart from the traditional atomic structure of the book: the page view.

And this is where I think we need to shift the terms of the debate. What matters is not the ability to add links or visual or audio content. This strikes me as just a departure from, not an enhancement of, reading. Rather, what should be at stake is how we may or may not reconceptualize the *formal structure* of reading. That is why reflecting on the nature of the page, rather than just the technology, is so important. It is the text's architecture, its structural details, that play as much a role in shaping our reading experiences as the underlying material profile of the book or screen. Only when we reconceptualize the page as the basic unit of reading are we truly entering into new conceptual terrain.

If our relationship to holding texts and looking at texts will be two of the features that will change most dramatically in the years to come as reading moves from pages to screens, our relationship to the "page" as the fundamental interface of text is also on the verge of potentially undergoing a categorical shift. It bears reflecting on what pages have done and what we would do without them.

First, pages.

Pages are windows. Pages allow us to look through, to trans-port ourselves into an imaginative space off the page. The use of marginal illustrations (fig. 3.2), the width of blank margins, the degree of whiteness of the page (which is never truly white), the shape of typefaces, and the distances between letters and words—all play a role in facilitating fenestration. But so does the text. Scenes of sleeping, dreaming, meandering, tinkering, and distant viewing (hilltops or cityscapes) are all descriptive techniques of having us see through something. When Virginia Woolf writes of Mrs. Ramsay in *To the Lighthouse*, "And she waited a little, knitting, wondering, and slowly those words they had said at dinner, 'the China rose is all abloom and buzzing with the honey bee,' began washing from side to side of her mind rhythmically,"[6] I know to let my mind wander, too, to see through the page before me, to enter into the world of Mrs. Ramsay's drifting mind as I then drift back to my own.

Pages are frames. Pages not only allow us to look through, but also at, to see something that has been distilled. Pages are like microscopes, only in reverse. They reduce the world to some-thing comprehensible. Unlike cinema screens, pages are smaller than the world they represent. When the twentieth-century Swiss writer Robert Walser began writing short stories in microscript while residing in a sanitarium, he was trying to find a way to capture this smallness of writing. Pages are an attempt to grasp that which is around us, to bring it down to size, to order it, and finally to save it. As Susan Orlean wrote about her orchid thief, so too of the page: "There are too many ideas and things and people. Too many directions to go. I was starting to believe the reason it matters to care passionately about something, is that it whittles the world down to a more manageable size."[7] Pages

[FIGURE 3.2] The Prayer Book of Kaiser Maximilian I (1513) was one of the most important illustrated books of the early sixteenth century and included marginal illustrations by artists such as Albrecht Dürer, Lucas Cranach the Elder, and Albrecht Altdorfer, among others. Folio 56v is reproduced here courtesy of the Bayerische Staatsbibliothek, München.

are signs of passion. They whittle, like sculptures with the excess marble chipped away.

We have developed many ways of framing reading over the ages: columns, headpieces, illuminated letters, footnotes, and of course punctuation are all ways of bringing words into focus. The introduction of spacing between words in the seventh century, the gradual standardization of punctuation and spelling in the seventeenth century (the great age of dictionaries), or even the vogue in the nineteenth century for presenting classics in double columns (the book as the new pantheon)—these are so many ways of arguing for the orderliness of reading amid the cacophony of texts.[8] So too is the age-old technique of ekphrasis, of focusing on a single object through the act of description. Description, which is a problem for narratologists (what *happens* when we describe something?), is a way of focusing our attention. It is a verbal form of punctuation. When Balzac writes of a Parisian gambling house, "The various salons are teeming with spectators and players; indigent old men who shuffle along in search of warmth; tormented faces belonging to those whose orgies began in wine and will end up in the Seine,"[9] this is a world I can know all at once. He has made Paris graspable for me two centuries later and an ocean away.

Pages are individuations. No matter how large or small, pages are finite. Unlike scrolls, pages are material arguments of individualization. We cannot read the recto and verso sides of the page at the same time (although we can intimate that more is to come when the ink bleeds through). As in Augustine's *Confessions*, pages allow us to access the world at random, out of sequence, as a piece.[10] Chapter headings (but not running headers), page numbers (but not gathering signatures), stanzas, paragraph breaks, and the numbering of verses are all forms of individuation. So too are rhetorical devices like synecdoche, where the part stands for the whole, and narrative devices like direct speech, which carves the world into different voices. Quotation marks, which came into use in the sixteenth century in France and the seventeenth century in England, are to the page as the page is to the book. As Marjorie Garber has written in her study of quotation marks, the duplication of quotation also implies a duplicity, a taking out of context—quotation marks are the grammatical seams of any text.[11]

Pages are mirrors. Although we may not be able to read recto and verso of the same page together, we can read them across opposing pages. Like books, pages are always double. As Garret Stewart has reminded us, "Every book is a diptych."[12] Pages face each other; they comment, reflect, illustrate, or confound one another. The scroll is constitutionally singular, one long sheet. Like the filmstrip or the tape spool, it may be comprised of parts sewn together, but the act of splicing is designed to cover over these differences, not highlight them. There is a seamlessness to the scroll that is not true of the book, whose spine is both anatomically and visually prominent. The page is always part of a "gathering," the book the sum of smaller versions of itself. The page argues for a logic of iterability, of sameness with a difference. It is this ability to mirror, to be like, that was behind the long-standing idea of the "book of nature," that the book could be a faithful reflection of nature and that nature was like a book. But also ourselves. In one of the most cherished Romantic novels written in German, *Heinrich von Ofterdingen* (1802), we see how the hero discovers a book in a cave that tells the story of his own life. Deep in the caverns of the book, *Heinrich von Ofterdingen* wants us to know, we see ourselves.

Pages are folds. The page is not just a part, but always a part of. It is a *folded* sheet, or else it would be a broadside, poster, or playbill. The essence of the page is the turn. With books reading is experienced as a gradual unfolding. The "foldout" is one of the most popular devices in the history of the book. Whether as a map, a table, a facsimile of a handwritten letter, or a pop-up world in a children's book, pages are imagined to unfold in our hands (fig. 3.3). They convey a sense of the development of readerly

[FIGURE 3.3] Lothar Meggendorfer was one of the great innovators in children's book design at the end of the nineteenth century. Here we see a facsimile of one of his most popular works, *Internationaler Circus* (1887). Image courtesy of the Rare Books and Special Collections Division, McGill University Library. © Esslinger Verlag, J. F. Schreiber GmbH, Esslingen/Germany.

thought. However much we like to remind ourselves that books are the first random access machines, there is still a remarkable degree of sequentiality to the technology of the page. In this, pages mirror the growth of nature around us (not to mention language). As Goethe remarked, "Nature can only achieve all that it can in a series. She does not make leaps."[13] This is one of the reasons that we have spoken of leaves and pages so interchangeably.

Taken all together, then, the book is an amalgam of the arbitrary, the simultaneous, and the sequential. Proust might be said to be its ultimate theorist. He takes the scattered associations of thought and puts them in order, an order that is always bursting at the seams. To lose a sense of sequence, no matter how complex, is ultimately to lose sense. That is why Proust's novel of soporific associations, a work that can only truly be understood at night, begins with the pathway, but also the parallel—the choice to go Swann's way or the Guermantes's way. As the anthropologist André Leroi-Gourhan has reminded us, the evolution of the human species was intimately tied to increasing degrees of sequential sophistication in tool cutting.[14] No matter how much we are drawn today to the horizontality (and democracy) of distributed cognition, we will always need sequence. Pathways allow us to do things over again, they are technologies of recurrence, perfectibility, and survival. Books, stories, *recounting* are primordial defenses against extinction.

+ +

The digital page, by contrast, is a fake, a simulation called up from distributed data.[15] It is not *really* there. The digital page could always be otherwise. It is this ludic aspect of the digital that was one of its most attractive features for early proponents. But what interests me is how the page might itself be otherwise. How might the plane of digital presentation move out of the realm of fakery and embrace its inner self, if it has one?

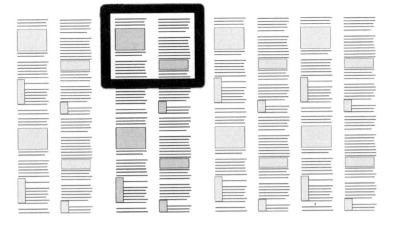

[FIGURE 3.4]   Craig Mod, "Books in the Age of
the iPad" (2011). Courtesy of the artist.

Roaming. If one of the crucial features of the page is its finitude—
that it stops—then one of the first ways to think beyond the
page is to transgress its horizontal limits. As an innovative new
voice in text design, "Craig Mod," has suggested, we can begin
to imagine texts not as stacked pages but as potentially infinite
planes (fig. 3.4).[16] Text no longer draws its inspiration from its
etymological origins of weaving, but instead from the shape of
the "pad" (Apple, as always, helping us see the shape of technology). According to this model, the reading device would remain
a lens, much like the page, but now the textual surface is roamable rather than turnable. One of the pleasures of reading the
printed page has historically been the way the eye can wander
across the page, the way we can take in different parts of the
text according to our own plan. Roamable text expands this
principle to ever greater dimensions, as reading devices become
tools of mobilization rather than iteration. Reading becomes nomadic rather than domestic. Where we "curl up" with a book,
we "roam" across a plane. Unlike the branching pathways of
links whose routes are difficult to visualize (who has not gotten

lost clicking through the web?), the plane seems more navigable to me. It insists on the knowledge of adjacency. There can be no jumping across the plane, as in a book or a hypertext; one must pass through something on the way to something else. Reading assumes a topological structure, one that was latent in the printed page (or even hypertext), but that becomes even more central in understanding the reading "plane." In learning how to roam, we are initiated more consciously, perhaps more critically, into the nature of our interconnected textual universe.

Zooming. Of all the technologies that have changed how we see our world, the satellite is surely one of the most important.[17] Google Earth is the popularized version of the satellite view. For all of its reputation as a search engine, I think one of Google's most significant contributions is the way it has changed how we visualize information, the way zooming has been irreversibly integrated into our understanding of both space and text. If roaming expands the horizontal edges of the page, zooming bursts through the page's two-dimensionality.[18] It returns us to the realm of microscopy, but perhaps also to the foldout or pop-up. Rather than release us into another space—the traditional dreamscape of the book—zooming suggests a constant quest for the beneath. Like Facebook, there is a preformationist logic at work here, as though everything is contained within everything else. It is only a matter of following the path downward, which is also a path backward to the beginning. Zoomtext has a genetic quality about it.

Aya Karpinska's *Shadows Never Sleep* (2009), a recent enchanting example of what she calls "a zoom narrative" (fig. 3.5), is a telling example of the way such digital drilling down is indebted to the association of reading and interiority that emerged out of the eighteenth century and whose most poignant symbol, as we saw in the last chapter, was the silhouette. Karpinska's whimsical text boxes of cutout images show us the way sentences have become pixilated, divorced from their normal grammar in the same way that the digital page is no longer connected to the spine of the book. But her choice of words is also a reminder of

[FIGURE 3.5] Aya Karpinska, *Shadows Never Sleep* (2009). Courtesy of the artist.

how this new art of discovery is tied to a sense of the anxiety that belonged to childhood. In a world of zooming we are always peering "in corners," "under the bed," "beneath the pillow." As with young children, there is a beneath or behind to all things. In Karpinska's evocative terms, we "stretch and shudder, whip and creep." When Walter Benjamin wrote his brief memoir of growing up in Berlin, he spoke of how children have a special knowledge of a home's corners (not for nothing was a popular German folk hero called "Faithful Eckhart," *Ecke* being the German word for corner). Like the little paper cutout dolls in Karpinska's *Shadows Never Sleep*, zoomtext returns us to a state of such childlike knowledge of the recess. It is a world filled with curiosity and wonder, but also disorientation, nervousness, and superstition. It suggests the way life online lends itself toward feelings of conspiracy and heteronomy—of being acted upon, the inverse of the book's imagined autonomy.

Streaming. One of the most important aspects of the page is its stability. When I turn it, it doesn't disappear (unless it rips and we all know how traumatic that is). But much writing today takes the form of what David Gelernter has called "lifestreams" (blogs, feeds, tweets, etc.), similar to the "Prayer Companion" used by the nuns in York, England, that streams statements gathered from the web that begin with the words, "I feel."[19] This kind of digital writing is by definition *en route*; it both comes and goes. Just as the page argues for its structural iterability—you can have as many as you like in one book (up to a point)—it also argues for the same principle at the level of experience. You can keep reading the same page over and over again (again, up to a point). Indeed the institutional study of literature, which for many is anathema to the pleasure of reading, is premised on this idea of rereading. Streams, on the other hand, are defined by their ephemerality. You can never step in the same one twice.

Writers for millennia have dreamed of writing as a stream. It is a means of imagining our way past the discrete nature of the book or the letters of the alphabet. In place of the isolated character there would be nothing but flow, what the poet Friedrich Hölderlin called "the streaming word." Or as Emily Dickinson wrote:

Tell all the Truth, but tell it slant—
Success in Circuit lies.[20]

The book, in all its finiteness, could never accommodate such dreams of fluidity. We still lack a satisfactory interface that would allow us to engage, pass on, and then let go of the new information streams. We have spent so much time worrying about the transience of digital texts—that unlike books they seem so impermanent—we have forgotten to install techniques of forgetting them, too. The point of Twitter is not to store it, as the Library of Congress has recently begun to do, but to create efficient means of letting it go, to embrace a kind of writing (and reading) that is expirable. What would be the best way to visualize writing as a stream and not as a plane or page?

+ +

This past week my son was home sick from school. Like most parents, I let him go on the computer so I could get a few things done. When I went down to see what he was doing, I found him "reading" Lego building instructions. There are much worse things he could have discovered, and again like most parents we've learned the hard way not to allow any unchaperoned time online anymore. He's five and although he cannot read yet, there he was meticulously making his way through "page" after "page" of a PDF file he had downloaded (how he had learned this I have no idea) of some extremely lethal flying machine. One by one he studied the pages upon which shapes were coming together to produce more complex shapes, overseen by the large bold numbers in the upper right hand corner of each page.

As we learned in the last chapter about the visual nature of reading, the building instructions that so fascinated my son mirror in many ways how we construct letters from more elementary shapes. Alphabet and architecture are closely related domains. It is no coincidence that his interest in these booklets corresponds to the very year in which he is beginning to learn to make the shape of letters himself (a process that is difficult for him and that I will return to in the next chapter). But equally important is the sequentiality of it all, the way number and letter coalesce in a constructive process. Much recent research suggests that counting, a number sense, precedes language, rather than the other way around as was previously thought.[21] A notion of order, magnitude, and succession may underlay our ability to use language, the cognitive precondition of that famed idea of universal grammar. My son's love of building instructions tells us something important about the intimate relationship between sequence and knowledge, whether it be literate or arithmetic.

As we think about designing new reading interfaces in the future, I hope we can begin to move past the boundaries of the page, to stop faking it so to speak. Nothing seems more misguided than creating websites that are meant to look like books or books that are meant to look like websites. If one day, in the words of Walter Scott's fictional publisher, there are simply too many pages and paper costs too much to continue to make books, then we might want to impersonate the book online. Until then, I hope we continue to think beyond the page.

But on a deeper level, reviewing the list of digital alternatives above reveals the way these new forms of reading preserve, albeit in altered form, a basic aspect of seriality that belonged to the printed page, and of course the scroll before it. The logic of the page was that of the fold and the turn; it was both unique and serially adjacent to what followed, which was also structurally similar. In each of the cases above, whether roaming, zooming, or streaming, we continue to move serially, only in new ways—we zoom through, roam past, or stream by. As Nietzsche said of man, "Regardless of where he lives, the desert and the cave are always with him," and presumably, so too is the stream.[22]

The successful reading interfaces of the future, whether handwritten, print, or digital, will ideally continue to preserve this sense of the "pathway." It is one of the oldest forms of human understanding, where mental thought mirrors how we make our way physically through the world. Unlike the so-called information superhighway, on the pathway (or even the road) I am aware of where I am, of moving through space. The truth of this sentiment is reflected not only in the deep anthropological record of toolmaking or the more recent cognitive experiments from the psych lab. It is also there in the way it forms the core of one of our most recurringly popular genres of storytelling, the road narrative. From the picaresque wanderings of Encolpius in the first century *Satyricon* to Lazarillo de Tormes in the sixteenth century, to the accidental urgency of Jack Kerouac in the twentieth, to the cinematically inspired digital work of Young-Hae Chang's *Dakota* at the opening of the twenty-first century, passing through space mirrors our passage through time and, ultimately, through thought. I want my children to learn how to learn one thing after another, to accept that there is a before and an after in life. I think reading books is still one of the best ways we have of reminding us of this fact. As Goethe once remarked, "It would be a lowly art that allowed itself to be understood all at once."[23]

FOUR

Of Note

Once as I looked up I saw a big, pure drop of rain slip from
leaf to leaf of a clematis vine. The thought occurred to me
that it was just such quick, unexpected, commonplace,
specific things that poets jot down in their note-books.

WALLACE STEVENS

Reading is born from writing, but it also begets more writing.
Reading is not only synonymous with dreaming (or sleepwalking), it can also be extractive. When we read, we take, we transform, we *do*. This is what we call taking notes. The verb is important to the noun's meaning. Not all of these notes, of course,
will become more writing. But writing almost always begins as
notes. Notes are an essential part of the economy of reading.
They are translational at their core, like the ribosomes of human
thought.

With the recent publication of Vladimir Nabokov's final, incomplete novel, *The Original of Laura* (2008), readers were offered a timely reminder of the tangled relationship between books
and notes. All that remained of Nabokov's "novel" at the time of
his death was a stack of index cards left in a safe. The book that
they became consisted of pages of perforated color facsimiles
of note cards with printed transcriptions beneath. There was
something profoundly disjunctive between the cards, the kind
that anyone could buy at a drugstore, and the weightiness of the

book to which they belonged, the last remaining novel by one of the twentieth-century's greatest writers.

In its affectionate reproduction of the authors' note cards in book form, *The Original of Laura* performed, at both a visual and tactile level, what we might call a morphological theory of media—that notes could become books, indeed that these two very different forms of writing (the cheapness of the index card and the majesty of the book) might be synonymous with one another. But in the cards' perforation—one of the most inspired publishing decisions of our so-called late age of print—the note cards' possible removal from the book also drew attention to the hole in the book…that was the note (fig. 4.1). Without notes, so *Laura* tells us, we have no books.

"So where is *Faust?*" a French visitor once asked Goethe. It was a question that would plague him his entire life. In reply Goethe is said to have dumped a sack of notes onto the table, declaring, "voilà mon Faust."[1] Some forty years later, Samuel Taylor Coleridge began publishing the "marginalia" from his books in *Blackwood's Magazine*, later popularized across the Atlantic by Edgar Allen Poe in the *Democratic Review*. In the first half of the twentieth century, Walter Benjamin created one of the greatest scholarly monuments of the modern period, *The Arcades Project*, consisting of an enormous collection of file folders of notes. The postwar writer Arno Schmidt began keeping his writing in elaborate note-card cases (fig. 4.2), from which would emerge bibliographic monstrosities like his elephantine novel *The Dream of Notes* (1970). More recently, Ann Carson in *Nox* (2010) has reimagined the book as a box containing one long foldout card of facsimiles of notes about her recently deceased brother. And there is a new website, Things in Books, that records the scraps of paper (and much more) found in books across the world. However diverse these projects may be, they are all different ways that individuals over the past two centuries have explored the relationship between the technology of the note and that of the book, to understand how our notes grow into, out of, alongside, or simply in our books.

[FIGURE 4.1] Vladimir Nabokov, *The Original of Laura (Dying Is Fun)*, edited by Dmitri Nabokov. © 2009 Dmitri Nabokov. Used by permission of Alfred A. Knopf, a division of Random House, Inc. Reproduced by permission of Penguin Books Ltd.

In thinking about the relationship between notes and books, and the various movements between them, I want to think about what happens today when our notes and books increasingly belong to the same medium. Of course we will continue, in Wallace Stevens's word, to "jot" down ideas on random slips of paper, as Goethe did on theater notices while drafting the last novella of his life or Melville did on a library call slip while taking notes for *Billy Budd*.[2]

But I think it is fair to say that for many of us much of our

[FIGURE 4.2]   Arno Schmidt, note-card case. Photo by Friedrich
Forssman. © Arno Schmidt Stiftung, Bargfeld, Germany.

note taking is done on the same medium as our book writing
and—this is where our current moment strikes me as crucially
different—*our book reading*. For medieval scholars, this would
have been the case as they moved from one manuscript sheet to
another in the reading, copying, and commenting that comprised
their notationally filled days. But since the invention of printing
there has been an essential schism between note taking and book
reading. It is this schism that interests me. As we gradually move
to a bookish world that is no longer exclusively defined by the
printed book (if it ever was), what happens to this lost sense of
metamorphosis surrounding composition—when "all is note" we
might say? What happens, in other words, to handwriting?

It may seem odd to think about the future of handwriting in
relation to the *printed* book. Print, after all, was the technology
that was supposed to have replaced handwriting. And yet one
of the unique features of printed books, and print media more
generally, has been their ability not only to coexist with manu-

script, but to *coproduce* a variety of handwritten practices in the form of marginalia, dedications, commonplace books, diaries, handwriting manuals, private letters about books, or even signatures (in the case of checks and passports).[3] Far from replacing manuscript, it turns out that print has been one of the great engines for keeping handwriting alive. It is this mutuality, this interdependence between handwriting and print, that seems to be one of the key stakes in the move to digital forms of reading. The future of reading, in other words, is connected with how we have understood the value of handwriting as readers.

+ +

"In taking these notes, I'm trusting myself to the banality that is in me," writes Roland Barthes in his notebook after the death of his mother.[4] Notes are, first and foremost, records of the quotidian. They are like the basements of our ideas, cluttered, yet full of useful things. "Paid $2.50 for cutting &c: the old tree in front," writes Walt Whitman in one of his notebooks.[5] He even wrote it down twice. In Susan Sontag's notebooks, now held in the special collections of the University of California, Los Angeles, we find vocabulary lists along with more memorable musings (such as meeting Thomas Mann).[6] Notes are where the often mind-numbing, repetitive mundaneness of our daily lives bump into the high-flying acrobatics of human intellect. As the poet James Merrill wrote about his notebooks, "The thought of so many opposing impulses sleeping peacefully face-to-face when the book is shut, remains oddly satisfying."[7] Not only satisfying, I suspect, but in those cohabitating, slumbering thoughts of the poet there undoubtedly lies a spark of creativity. Notes are like silent embers.

Notes are also meant to be fast, capturing those "quick, unexpected, commonplace, specific things," in Wallace Stevens's words, like a raindrop sliding down a clematis vine. Or as Mary Oliver jotted down in one of her notebooks:

Something totally unexpected,
like a barking cat.[8]

Swiftness and unexpectedness go hand in hand with notes. As Stendhal wrote in a note on the messiness of his handwriting: "<u>Writing</u>: this is how I write when my thoughts are treading on my heels. If I write well, I waste them."[9] For great note takers the suddenness of the note is the precondition of new ideas, possibly the *great* idea. In Joyce's notebooks to *Finnegans Wake*, the first of which he called "Scribbledehobble," we see one case after another of flashes of insight into the nature of language: "pass the grass / behush the bush," "muchrooms," or the unsurpassable, "nutsnolleges."[10]

In the note's speed, we dream of immediacy, of a place where there is no longer a gap between our thoughts and the words on the page. In the seventeenth century, the age of great diarists like Samuel Pepys, handbooks on tachygraphy, or "short-writing," were all the rage. As an admirer wrote at the opening of William Hopkins's *The Flying Pen-Man, or The Art of Short Writing* (1674):

> For what are Diamonds whilst in the Rocks,
> Lock'd up so close in Nature's secret Box?
> What's Art entomb'd within a private breast?
> Like Love and Light: diffuse it and increas't.[11]

For the late Victorians, photography was imagined to be the new medium capable of solving the problem of the instantaneity of thought, bypassing the stenographic note altogether. Louis Darget, member of the Society for the Study of Supernormal Pictures, pioneered the genre of the "thought photograph," taking unexposed plates and pressing them to the foreheads of sitters. We are forever on the paradoxical hunt for technologies that allow us to communicate without them.

Notes not only let us go fast, they also allow us to look over our ideas in some distilled fashion. Notes are technologies of oversight. Goethe was famous for creating vast charts prior to writing. Synopsis was a key antecedent to narration, the visualization of writing an essential step in the creative process. In the work of his contemporary Stendhal, whose autobiography, *The Life of Henry Brulard* (1835–36), remained unpublished (yet bound) at the time of his death, numerous pages were covered with topographical drawings from Stendhal's childhood. The visual is deeply specific, perhaps comically so in Stendhal, in ways that language never could be. "I could write a volume on the circumstances of the death of someone so dear," Stendhal writes on the occasion of his mother's death when he was a young boy. "That's to say, I know nothing whatsoever of the details."[12] In his visual rendering of the event, by contrast, all is detail (fig. 4.3). The sense of scale, the domestic labels, and the numbered annotations—"1) my father in his armchair, 2) fireplace, 3) M. Pison"—are the graphical poles to writing's looseness.

As the proliferation of schemas, lists, or maps tell us, perhaps one of the most important aspects of the note is this visual element. As Samuel Coleridge writes in his notebooks, "Without drawing I feel myself but half invested in language."[13] Notes allow us to bring words and images together, to write and envision at the same time. "Word and image are correlates that eternally search for one another," suggests Goethe in one of his many aphorisms.[14] Peruse the notebooks of Leonardo, Michelangelo, or Goethe and you will witness the deep complementarity of drawing and writing, the beauty, spark, and curiosity of intermedial thought.

Notes may be deeply visual, but they are also good for cancellation.[15] They allow us to see something disappear. Notes are vanishing points, a place where we undo our ideas, an integral part of the lost and found of reading. "Marginalia are deliberately pencilled," writes Poe, "because the mind of the reader wishes to unburthen itself of a *thought*."[16] Or as Coleridge writes in his notebooks, "Half a page wasted in Nonsense, and a whole page in the confutation of it. But such is the nature of exercise—I walk a mile for health—& then another to return home again."[17]

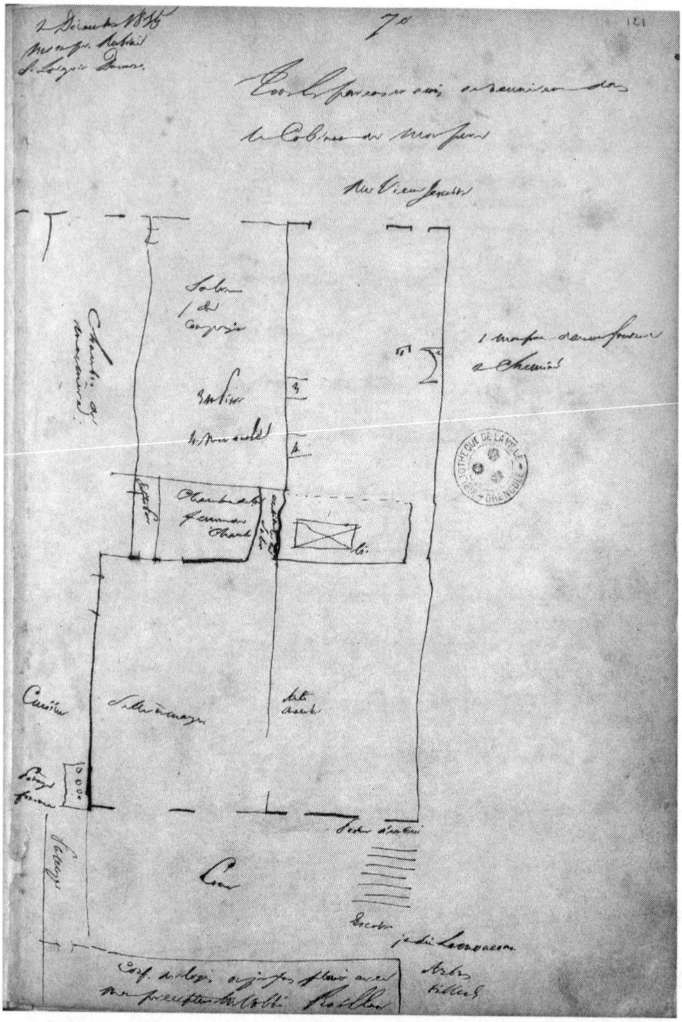

[FIGURE 4.3] In this drawing Stendhal reconstructs his family home at the time of his mother's memorial, labeling each of the rooms ("my mother's bedroom," "reception room," "small room," "kitchen," "bed") as well as the position of people within them ("1. my Father in his armchair," "2. fireplace," "3. M. Pison," "4. my uncle"). Stendhal, *Vie de Henry Brulard* (1835–36), 1:248. Courtesy of the Bibliothèque Municipale de Grenoble, France.

Notes are like exercise, the systole and diastole, the in and out, of thought.

The most iconic symbol of such "unburthening" thought has been that indispensable handwritten sign, the scribble. Nabokov may have achieved the apex of this art of cancellation in a note included in *Laura*, in which we see him working through a list of synonyms for the word "erasure" (efface, expunge, delete, rub out), where one of the words is itself scribbled out. As the Enlightenment satirist and natural scientist Georg Lichtenberg remarked in his collection of aphorisms, *The Waste-Books*, "With many a work of a celebrated writer I would rather read what he has crossed out than what he has let stand."[18] There is a subtle difference between the cross-out—where what is underneath is still legible, as in Joyce's notebooks to *Finnegans Wake*—and the scribble proper, where, as in Nabokov, the idea is fully blocked from view, but not the fact of its once having been thought. No matter how much our hard drives can preserve our writing in multiple different states, it still seems a far cry from the layering of assertion and cancellation made possible by the handwritten note.

Then there is the notation that is not a cancellation of an idea one has already had, but a placeholder for an idea one hopes might come. In the notebooks of Walt Whitman we see him working on his evocative poem "Crossing Brooklyn Ferry," where he writes, "I too have— —/ have— have—/ I too have— — — felt the curious questioning come upon me."[19] In the notebooks of the Romantic naturalist turned novelist Achim von Arnim, we see an inkblot from his notes on electricity that is gradually transformed into a rather comical image of a Phoenix (one that looks more like a turkey).[20] Handwritten lines lead us on to new thoughts and visions, they are premonitions, like Whitman's poetry, of what is (hopefully) to come.

If notes are signs of ourselves at our most intimate (hopeful, vacuous, diffuse), they can also be records of thoughts not our own. Notes can record those chance musings we overhear in the course of our day and that we could never invent on our own, like F. Scott Fitzgerald who wrote down in his notebooks the crass and dreamy words of his age:

> Bijou, regarding her cigarette fingers: "Oh, Trevah! Get me the pumice stone."[21]

Then there is the commonplace book, which consists of words copied down from our reading and which took off in the Renaissance under the tutelage of Erasmus and is still very much with us. In the sixteenth century, commonplacing was a way of learning the art of rhetoric, of how classical authors thought and spoke so that young readers might learn to do the same.[22] The posterior nature of the note, the way it came after reading, was also preparatory, to get us ready for something else. Never simply rhetorical, the copying of commonplaces was a way of understanding the world, of breaking it down into orderable parts. As Philipp Melanchthon remarked in his *De locis communes*, "Do not think commonplaces are to be invented casually or arbitrarily: they are derived from the deep structures of nature."[23]

Sometimes, though, we don't copy, we just jot down ideas right there on the page in front of us. This is the difference between notation and annotation, between the before, the after, and the simultaneous. Scholars like Heather Jackson, Anthony Grafton, and William Shermann have given us marvelous histories of the things people have written down in the margins of their books.[24] Who would not want to know what Ben Jonson thought of Chaucer (Jonson drew a long flower by the lines, "For he that truly loves servant is, / Were lother be shamed than to die") or Virginia Woolf of James Joyce ("No one has any wish to abuse the ancients").[25]

But as the book historian Leah Price has reminded us, perhaps books mark us most when we don't mark them.[26] In Herman Melville's copy of Dante's *Divine Comedy*, which was translated by Henry Francis Cary under the title *The Vision* in 1814, we find copious amounts of marginal notes. But there is one canto of the

Inferno that curiously lacks all marginalia: Canto 26, the tale of Ulysses, the great maritime adventurer, who begins his story:

> Forth I sail'd
> Into the deep illimitable main,
> With but one bark...[27]

Three years after buying Cary's Dante, Melville would complete *Moby Dick* (1851). The absence of annotation was, in this case, not a sign of distraction. It was an indication of a reader's most profound identification with his reading. At some point, we must put the pen down.

+ +

Today, there is no lack of note-taking software out there. Indeed, you could say we live in a golden age of notes. Devonthink allows you to search algorithmically for clippings you've pasted from your reading, a kind of desktop-sized Google. Collex allows you to annotate online objects located in archives or digital repositories and repurpose them to produce your own personal collections and exhibits. Jotspot, now Google Sites, allows users to create collaborative work spaces, from family websites to corporate projects. The iPad has a bookmarks feature that allows you to save all your underlinings (though not annotations) from your reading, and the Sony and Kindle e-readers save annotations as separate, downloadable files. PDF programs like Adobe have elaborate markup features, and Microsoft's "track changes" has proven remarkably successful for collaborative authorship. Indeed, one could argue that the web itself is just a giant notepad, where every text is by definition annotated in "hypertext markup language." Blogs are not only like electronic diaries, they also have a commentary function, making them a hybrid between medieval and modern books. Your hard drive, too, will save everything you write in multiple states, essentially a sprawling notebook of unfinished business. And then there is LivePen, which sucks up your notes into its internal memory and saves them to your desktop as PDF files. It gives a whole new meaning to the inhalation of ideas.

Almost all of the features of note taking I described in the first section about handwriting are thus replicable, if not improvable, with digital software. We can type faster than we can write with our hands; no collection of commonplaces could be more heterogeneous, yet potentially orderable than our hard drives; synoptic tables are easier than ever to construct; digital devices record better, whether acoustically or typographically through functions like copy and paste; and we can still annotate our texts, just like in the margins of our books. And by creating annotations as separate files, the digital synthesizes commonplacing and marginalia in a single act.

This leaves us with just one, but perhaps deeply significant, difference: handwriting. As Melville urged in his novel *Pierre, or the Ambiguities*: "But the handwriting, Pierre,—they want the sight of your hand!"[28] In a world of increasingly mass-produced texts, handwriting mattered in the nineteenth century. Albums of autographs, dedication leaves within Gift Books, and of course letters (more and more letters) were increasingly popular as the century wore on, various ways of preserving the image of handwriting alongside the widespread mechanization of writing.

The question is, does handwriting still matter? In a world of digital interfaces that are themselves remarkably successful in transcoding most, if not all, of our motley note-taking practices (right down to the signature which can be algorithmically reconfigured), is there any value left to the handwritten?

For many readers, the answer is clearly yes. We are treated to a regular volley of lamentations over the death of handwriting in the popular press these days, no less numerous than those assailing the death of the book.[29] (Their mutual frequency should tell us something about their codependence as media.) And an ever-growing body of research concerns the cognitive benefits of handwriting and drawing, of crafting symbols with one's hand rather than a keyboard. Nevertheless, handwriting, and especially cursive, is taught less and less in schools in the name of a new "keyboarding" mandate. While we have been here before (remember the typewriter?), handwriting's institutional future seems more up for grabs than ever before.

Much of the fervor surrounding handwriting was encapsulated in a thoughtful piece written in a small online magazine, *Good*, in which the scholar and writer Anne Trubek suggested that we should stop teaching handwriting altogether.[30] She received over 1,400 replies. Trubek's point was straightforward enough. Handwriting has historically been imbued, she argued, with a sense of class and moral privilege. Good penmanship was a sign of being a good person (and a man, as the gendered connotations of the word were important). A less "expressive" medium like typing would level the playing field, yet another way that new media often seem to have (or are thought to have) a democratizing effect. Teachers, after all, grade neatly written papers better than poorly written ones, privileging form over content and disadvantaging students who might have great ideas but face challenges with their motor skills. As Trubek tells us, this was the case with her son, once again gender being a salient piece of the story.

In addition to being "fairer," typing is also faster. It more closely aligns thinking with our writing, a latter day version of those Victorian thought photographs. Recent studies suggest that students who struggle with handwriting struggle with writing more generally as they progress through the educational system.[31] Difficulty with either the manual challenges of handwriting or the temporal disjunction between thought and expression can negatively impact students' future interest in the practice of writing. In the time it takes to master the cognitive-motor alignments of handwriting, we lose students along the way. If we dropped handwriting altogether, so Trubek, there would be no more discouraged writers, just confident typists.

Learning how to write with one's hands is indeed difficult. Nineteenth-century handbooks that tried to bring handwriting to the adult masses often provided suggestions about tying up one's body to produce the proper strokes.[32] As one researcher in the field of handwriting studies has suggested, "Using a pen is one of the most demanding and complex fine motor functions of humans involving movements of different parts of the arm and distinct grip force adjustments during movements."[33] So if it is so difficult, and if it does contribute to negative educational outcomes, why take the time to learn it? Why not teach typing earlier and abandon the laborious training of handwriting instruction altogether?

The first reason has to do with that embodied aspect that makes handwriting so difficult to learn in the first place. When contemporary commentators draw attention to the ability of digital media to replicate and improve upon note-taking devices like the commonplace book, they often highlight the generative value that resides in such practices. As the media theorist Steven Johnson has written on commonplacing, "When text is free to flow and combine, new forms of value are created."[34] For Johnson, today's textual aggregation software is like the commonplace book on a grand scale, one that generates new ideas through the act of repurposing. Its advantage is that it can do so more swiftly, more massively, and more "freely."

But in focusing solely on the outcome of commonplacing, we overlook the value of the *labor* of commonplacing, all that time spent copying other people's words with our hands. (There is a humorous moment in Johnson's piece when he suggests that digital texts appear "broken" if they cannot be copied. It never seems to occur to him that he could copy out the words on the screen by hand.) The point of commonplacing is not just combination, but repetition and, by extension, internalization. In copying the words of another writer word for word, early modern readers were learning how to internalize those words so that they could use them later on, in new ways and in new settings. As Erasmus remarked, comparing his readers to the popular symbol of the honeybee, "What bees bring back is not honey to start with. They turn it into liquid by the action of their mouths and digestive organs, and having transformed it into themselves, they then bring it forth from themselves."[35]

True creation for Erasmus begins with copying, with the duplication of existing knowledge. Otherwise it would lack substance. It requires that we know something of what has come before us. But true creation also begins with the *time* of copying, with the experience of incorporation, what Erasmus calls "digestion." Cutting and pasting is not the same as tracing letters with one's hand only faster. In forgoing the process of internalizing learning, of writing things down in one's soul, as Socrates said of conversation in the *Phaedrus*, we diminish our ability to create. True creation isn't the act of moving existing pieces around a board. It is about taking something in and transforming it. It is about taking time. For these thinkers, there is a great deal of knowledge encoded in the act of recreation.

But in learning to write with our hands, we are also learning a different *kind* of knowledge altogether. When we write with our hands we are also learning to draw, just as when we learn to draw we are learning to think more complexly with words. Research suggests that early elementary school students who draw before they write tend to produce more words and more complex sentences than those who do not.[36] And as historians of writing have shown, writing makes drawing more analytical. It allows for more complex visual structures and relations to emerge.[37] As Goethe remarked, word and image, drawing and writing, are correlates that eternally search for one another. Handwriting is an integral means of their convergence.

In the field of psychology there is a well-known experiment involving rats that tests their ability to coordinate different kinds of knowledge.[38] Rats are very good at navigating mazes and very good at recognizing color. What they cannot do is connect geometric information (left/right) with chromatic information (blue/red). Human cognition, by contrast, is premised on the idea of integrating these different domains of knowledge (whether such integration is modular or graded is up for debate). And it is language, so researchers surmise, that makes possible this communication between different mental faculties. What makes human knowledge unique—what makes humans human in other words—is this additive, multidimensional quality of thought. Drawing isn't just one more way of thinking. Drawing plus writing is a whole new *way* of thinking. It is where we become categorically different.

Handwriting is thus a valuable human skill because it is where our representation of the world is at its most multidimensional. Not only does it bring together the opposition between writing and drawing within a single practice. It also articulates a sense of difference beyond itself in relation to the typographic (either printed or electronic). This is why the recent rise of digital handwriting through the electronic stylus will likely remain so unsatisfying. Electronic conduction not only lacks the intimate precision of paper and pen (or pencil, crayon, and charcoal); it also loses handwriting's ability to preserve a sense of communicative difference from another medium. It loses an opportunity to think about the non-encodable and the non-transferable, the things that are lost when we change how we communicate.

In the Goethe archive, located in Weimar, Germany, one can find among the author's many papers two folio-sized sheets folded into fourths that belonged to the composition of the last novella of his life, which Goethe tellingly titled "Novella" (fig. 4.4). The archive where they are held is a hulking building that was constructed at the close of the nineteenth century, and it marked the beginning of a larger movement of creating spaces to house the manuscriptural remains of a nation's most famous writers. The preservation of handwriting, whether in the form of notes, letters, or diaries, had become an integral component not only for understanding a writer's published work, but for stabilizing a cultural heritage more generally. Today, we are once again seeing the establishment, or reestablishment, of authorial archives, this time in digital form. The process is repeating itself, though with an important difference. Where the paper archive affirmed the material differences of writing, the digital archive flattens

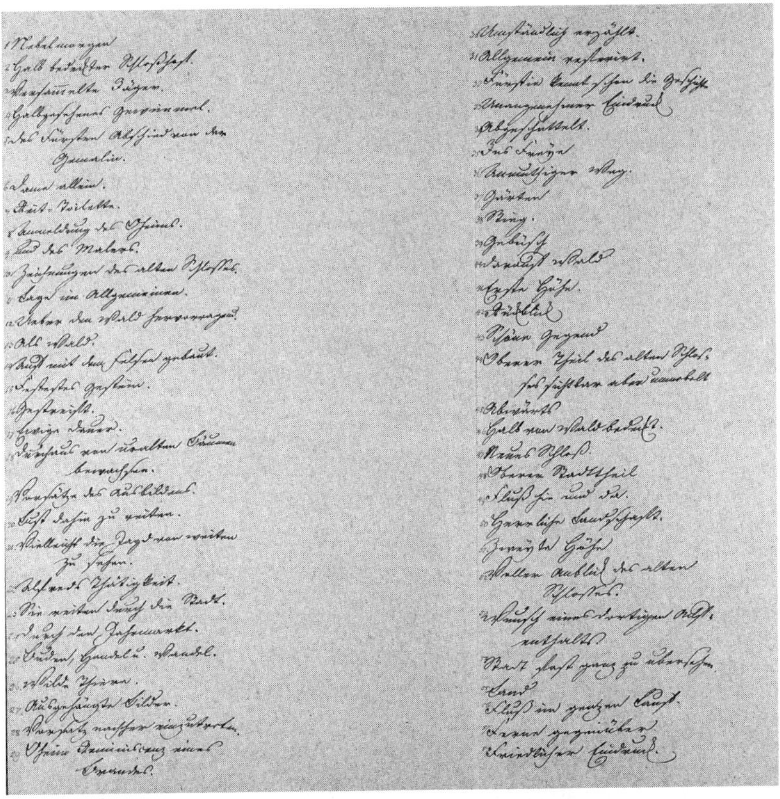

[FIGURE 4.4]   List of keywords related to Goethe's
last work of prose fiction, "Novella." Courtesy of the
Klassik Stiftung Weimar, GSA 25/W1992, Bl. 5.

everything into identical objects. In the digital archive, everything
is reduced to the status of a document.[39] The timelessness of the
paper archive, by contrast, was meant to redirect our attention
to the time and the process of writing.

Returning to Goethe's sheets, we can see how they consist of an
elegantly handwritten list of 107 numbered keywords that extend
down the first and third columns with the numbers written in red
ink and the words in black. The keywords were written down
by Goethe's secretary one morning as the author dictated them,

comprising the narrative framework of his novella, which was to be based on James Fenimore Cooper's *The Pioneers* (1823).

Such schematic columns were increasingly common to Goethe's late work, and in them we can see how important the act of synoptic visualization was for his thinking about narration. Oversight was the beginning of story (as was counting, a point I will return to in chapter 7). But in the beautifully finished state of the handwriting—called a "Reinschrift" or "fair copy"—the handwritten list of keywords is also supposed to be an end in itself. There is something superfluous to this note, a remainder that cannot be incorporated into the printed book that it will eventually become. This fact is beautifully on display (illegible in reproduction) in the way the handwritten columns are bounded by folds in the paper, a practice that was common to Goethe's note taking so that he or his scribe could subsequently add annotations, after which the list could be copied out again.

The note for Goethe was thus a consummate expression of differentiation: different from its author through the scribal hand; different from its future identity as a printed page through its calligraphic formality; and different to itself in the technique of the fold that divided presentation and annotation within a single leaf. In passing from note to book all of this was necessarily going to be left behind. And yet in its deliberate archival quality, it would still be legible to future readers—not just legible, but gorgeously, flagrantly, flamboyantly so, in order that we might one day understand how writing in books emerges through time. Nothing seemed to argue more forcefully for the morphological relationship between notes and books than this fair copy list of dictated keywords bounded by the fold.

Goethe's leaf shows us something important about the nature of writing, but also about what it means to think about nature. Where many of his contemporaries were at work incorporating the handwritten note *into* the printed page—making print more notelike as in Poe's printing of his marginalia or Novalis's equating the printed fragment with a kind of pollination—for Goethe notes were as much sediments as they were seeds. They showed us the differences that inhered in ideas and natural forms, the insurmountable remainders of life. As his American disciple, Ralph Waldo Emerson, would write, "The law of nature is alternation forevermore."[40]

+ +

As I write this, my son is sitting in the next room doing his homework for kindergarten, or "maternelle" as we call it here. It is a "fiche de lecteur," and he is supposed to write out the title by hand and draw a passage from the book I have just read him in my garbled French-Canadian accent. He routinely struggles with this assignment, both physically and emotionally (his three-year-old sister, meanwhile, is upstairs imitating him, shouting: "This is not barbouillage! [These aren't scribbles!]"). Where she seems indifferent to the judgment of others in the literally thousands of notes she leaves around the house in her imaginary script, because my son's letters and his drawings are not as good as many of the students in his class, he feels frustrated by the exercise, much like Trubek's son and, I am sure, many other boys in particular. I try to tell him that drawing is not about imitation, but expression, and we spend some time looking at books of modern art to make the point as visible as possible (needless to say this doesn't really work).

What I don't tell him is how important this struggle is. He is learning to draw while he learns to read, and he is learning to write while he learns to draw. All of those aspects are being bound together in his brain. Were we to let go of handwriting he would lose a key piece of this mental puzzle. Dissociating drawing, writing, and reading from one another would disempower some of his, and our, creative and cognitive potential—not to mention he would have one less tool at his disposal to convey his future self to another. There is a profound sense of person that comes through the work of one's hand that cannot fully be replicated digitally.

Perhaps most important, in learning to write with their hands, my son and daughter are learning to make those letters in the same way they are learning to make the figures when they draw. There is a craftsmanship, a carefulness, to letter writing (and drawing) that I do not want them to lose. Unlike typewritten letters, handwritten letters are constructions. It is this artisanal aspect of learning to write that is, to my way of thinking, one of the most important aspects of handwriting. Who would want to lose that as part of the saga of human creativity? Surely it is worth the effort.

In one of his earliest essays, Walter Benjamin suggested that the invention of the index card marked the end of the book.[41] Its stackability brought us back to the origins of writing and the three-dimensionality of the rune or knot-notation (a fact that curiously overlooks the book's actual geometry). But the book had also become superfluous for Benjamin because it was merely an in-between stage to the notes that we took down to write books and those we took from books (presumably to write more books). Instead of dispensing with handwriting, we could just dispense with the book. All would be note.

But what Goethe's handwritten leaf reminds us is that these acts of copying and differentiation are extremely significant for how we think. If we only ever move from notes on cards to more notes on cards or from notes on computers to more notes on computers, where will the sense of the morphology, the multi-dimensionality of ideas reside? As Nabokov's *The Original of Laura* so palpably showed us, there may be notes without books, but there cannot be books without notes. Perhaps one of the essential reasons for preserving the printed book is the way it argues for this transformational nature of writing—that writing, like thought, nature, and the self to which it gives expression, must be understood as a form that changes over time in order to capture the larger truth of who we are and the world we inhabit. Without these material articulations of serial difference, we lose a key piece of knowledge of the world and ourselves.

FIVE

Sharing

Sharing is more difficult than you think.

J. W. GOETHE [*the man of fifty*]

We not only keep books, but we also give them away. Books are some of the most important objects that we share with one another. We may largely read in isolation today, but we still wish for commonality when it comes to reading. This is part of the longing that is reading.

In the summer of 2010, the Concord Free Press published its first book, *Give and Take,* by Stona Finch, about a jazz pianist-cum-jewel thief. Instead of selling the book to readers, the press gave the book away for free. They asked readers for a donation—not to the press, but to a charity of their choice. They then requested that readers pass the book on to another reader when they were finished, who was asked to make a further charitable contribution in a great chain of giving. The book raised more than $40,000.

This is an important story, but not because it offers an example of the newly popular economics of "free."[1] After all, a lot of money changed hands. Rather, it highlights the rich history of how books have served as gift objects. In the ninth century, Charlemagne, the emperor of the Holy Roman Empire, bequeathed his entire royal library, one of the most impressive in all of medieval Europe, to be sold off and the proceeds given to the poor. In the nineteenth century, books were some of the most important gift items in the burgeoning industry known as Christmas.[2] In the wake of the Napoleonic wars, to take another example, the Prussian government created a lottery designed to raise money for the families of crippled soldiers. They did so by giving away books for every purchased ticket, an anthology of fiction and poetry by the day's leading writers. After World War I, Queen Mary did the same thing, creating a book "in aid of convalescent auxiliary hospitals for soldiers and sailors who have lost their limbs in the war."[3] Throughout their history books have been invested with an almost magical power to hold us together, or, as in the case of those returning soldiers, to piece us spiritually back together.

Reading is never purely an act of isolation. When we read, we enter into a world of commonality, whether of language, story, or material object. Reading socializes. "To us these marvelous tales have been told," begins the great medieval German epic *The Nibelungenlied*. Reading is about the constitution of some "us." If my previous chapters have been about the way we relate to reading as individuals—where reading serves as a form of individuation—this chapter is about the way we have reading in common, how we form social bonds through our reading material. The physicality of what we read is an integral part of this story. How different technologies facilitate or inhibit the act of sharing will be a key determinant not only of their future success, but of the way we think about reading.

Almost every major textual initiative today is structured around three overlapping notions of sharing: commonality, transferability, and sociability. We want other people to read the same thing we are reading (commonality); we want to be able to send other people what we are reading (transferability); and we want to be able to talk to other people about what we are reading (sociability). "Social reading" is shaping up to be the core identity, or ideology if you will, of digital media.

I say ideology because there is also something duplicitous about the new commitment to sharing. Never before has the proprietary relationship to reading and ideas been more in force.

Sharing texts has never been more popular—and illegal. As historians of copyright have reminded us, the initial idea of the *limited* nature of intellectual property that emerged in the eighteenth century, a kind of compromise between serving a common good and individual incentive, is becoming increasingly one-sided.[4] In a culture of licensing and digital rights management (DRM), owning is becoming absolute, while sharing is now the limited practice. Corporate interest is winning out over a sense of the history of human habit. What disappears is that common space that binds us together, where ideas are no longer yours or mine but ours.

But do we really understand what we mean by sharing or "social" media? The more inclined we are to see sharing as the solution to our increasingly restrictive landscape of intellectual property, the more I want to ask after sharing's nature. Rather than indulge in another, and as far as I can tell largely impotent, critique of copyright (roll on Disney, roll on), I am interested in thinking about the challenges of having reading in common. As the great historian of Renaissance gift practices Natalie Zemon Davis once argued, "We have concentrated on the book as a commodity rather than on the book as a bearer of benefits and duties, on copyright rather than common right."[5] When we debate copyright today, we often take for granted that we know what its opposite is, this thing called "common right."

My aim in this chapter is to bring into view how writers and readers of the past have thought about what it means to hold reading in common, and in particular how they have thought about the *difficulty* of sharing what one has read. One of the fundamental identities of book reading as it has emerged over time is the challenge it poses to producing a sense of commonality. Reading is a technique of socialization with a deeply asocial element. Virginia Woolf's well-known appeal to "the common reader" in her collections of essays in the early twentieth century was just one of the most famous examples of a steady appeal to commonality when it comes to reading. Such appeals are constant, one suspects, because never quite successful.

There are two camps emerging today in the reading wars: those who would defend the intellectual commons and those who would defend intellectual property. It's time to move beyond this oversimplified antagonism. Rather than rehearse arguments for and against, rather than announce that all is sharing despite a legal reality that flies in the face of such a pronouncement, we would do well to spend more time reflecting on what it means to hold ideas in common.[6] If there is such a thing as an intellectual "commons" or a "common reader" how did he, she, or it get there? What are the kinds of practices and technologies that make it possible to have reading in common, and what are the limitations? Can there be such a thing as too much sharing? As we share more and more with one another, will we conversely own less and less? Is sharing a licensed file of code the same as sharing a book? Can it even be called sharing if we don't actually give some *thing* away?

As we think about the future of reading, we will want to think about the history of how we have shared reading, the intricate and often troubled ways that individuals have parted, imparted, and parted with ideas. We will want to heed Goethe's advice that sharing is more difficult than we think.

+ +

In the Judeo-Christian tradition, the original act of sharing was not a book, but a bone. In Genesis 2:21–22, God makes Eve from a rib in Adam's body. This has most often been understood as an affirmation of patriarchal rule (she is of Adam in the way that he is of God). But it can also be read as a repayment for her bringing the gift of life into the world. Take something of him, the story implies, because you will henceforward share something of yourself. Sharing is a chain reaction; it always presupposes more of itself.

What is particularly interesting about this story is the object that is exchanged. At the core of this primal scene of human sharing is a bone, the most durable part of the human body, and also, it should be added, the oldest writing surface. Unlike the rest of our organic matter, bones endure; they far exceed the span of human life. They make possible knowledge between generations at a material level. Bones are an essential component in the shaping of human cultures. In the story of Adam and Eve, the sharing of a thing precedes the sharing of knowledge (in the famous tree from which Eve would soon eat). Things make the sharedness of ideas possible.

The parable of the rib is a reminder that genuine sharing involves some object—I must give something up in order for you to take something in. Sharing is not purely synonymous with giving, but it does belong to the same family.[7] Like a gift, there is a sense of sacrifice about sharing, as when a child learns to share a toy by giving it up temporarily. But unlike a gift, when I share something with you I also retain something else, something more ethereal like a bond of friendship or an idea that I hold on to. The rib is important to this story because as a bone there are more like it. In being given, something is also withheld. It is a part of me, but only a part. As a shared object, the rib is both internal and external to me. Only under these conditions can we, as two separate people, paradoxically enter into a common space of what Genesis calls "one flesh."

We might say that books are like bones. They too preserve ideas across generations. They too belong to a ritual of material and intellectual exchange. And they too consist of this mixture of the essential and the expendable. If we look at one of the most popular scenes involving books, the dedication of a book from an author to a royal or holy patron, I think we can see the logic of Genesis at work (fig. 5.1). As the great Renaissance naturalist Ulisse Aldrovandi hands a book to his patron, Pope Clementine the VIII, we can see the deep sense of disavowal enacted in the performance. In order to truly share a book with another, one must submit oneself before the recipient. Giving a book, according to this imagery, is a way of giving a piece of oneself. We lose something of ourselves when we share, but not everything (there are always more copies). Such scenes point to sharing's etymo-

[FIGURE 5.1]   Title page from Ulisse Aldrovandi, *Ornithologia* (1599).
Courtesy of the Landesbibliothek Württemberg, Stuttgart, Nat. G. fol. 16-1.

logical origins in the verb "to shear," as both a carving from and
an act of forking.

In his dedication to his patron, the Earl of Southampton,
Shakespeare writes at the opening of his poem *The Rape of Lu-
crece* (1594), "What I have done is yours, what I have to doe is
yours, being part in all I have, devoted yours."[8] One can part
with a work because the recipient is already a part of the author.
There is a sense of entanglement to the writing and reading of
books. When the ninth-century Benedictine monk Rabanus Maurus handed over a copy of his renowned poems of the cross to
the archbishop of Mainz—a copy we must remember that would
have taken him an entire year just to reproduce by hand—he is
depicted as being supported by his teacher, Alcuin of York, the
leading scholar of the court of Charlemagne (fig. 5.2). When
we give something of ourselves—our ideas, our time, our sense
of care—we expose ourselves, we become more vulnerable. Be-

hind every book is some support, in this case the support of a teacher.

At the turn of the sixteenth century, Erasmus would publish his famed collection of adages with the opening motto, "Friends hold all things in common."[9] The *Adages* ushered in a new way of thinking about reading as something held in common among friends (not to mention a new way of privatizing common intellectual property). Alongside the vertical supplication between author, patron, teacher, or divine muse, by the sixteenth century reading was increasingly being thought of within a horizontal

[FIGURE 5.2]   Rabanas Maurus (*left*) is supported by Alcuin of York (*middle*) as he hands his manuscript to the archbishop of Mainz (*right*) in the *Manuscriptum Fuldense* (ca. 831–40). Courtesy of the Österreichische Nationalbibliothek, Vienna, cod. 652, fol. 1v.

framework of equals. One of the most popular book formats of the age were *Alba amicorum*, or Friendship Albums, in which friends could write brief sentiments in each other's blank books. They were part of the itinerant nature of university life and are still a common practice today in the form of the "yearbook." As Walter Scott, Baron of Buccleuch and a distant relative to the famous nineteenth-century novelist by the same name, would write in George Strachan's album in 1603, "Friendship is to be worshipped above all else because it is so rare on earth."[10]

By the eighteenth century, friendship would become one of the primary signs under which poetry was written and circulated among circles of sentimental readers. As the most renowned German poet of the age, Friedrich Klopstock, would write in one of his most beautiful poems, "Lake Zurich":

> But sweeter still, more beautiful and beguiling,
> Is to be a friend knowingly in the arms of a friend.

Samuel Taylor Coleridge would one day begin a periodical called *The Friend*, while one of Emerson's best-known essays, "Friendship," was written in the spirit of his Renaissance predecessor Michel de Montaigne ("A friend may well be reckoned the masterpiece of nature," writes Emerson).[11] By the middle of the nineteenth century a new genre of books had emerged that were designed expressly to be given away as gifts among family and friends.[12] These so-called Gift Books bore names like *Friendship's Offering*, *The Token*, and *Pocket-Book for Love and Friendship*. They often contained elaborate presentation leaves to allow givers to inscribe their names within them. Today, "to friend" has become a verb.

When we share a book with a friend, we are declaring our attachment—to an object, an idea, and a person. Sharing is a way of going public. It is what transforms a private reading experience into a public act, however small or large such publics might be. By the eighteenth century this ideal of personal friendship surrounding reading began to assume more institutional shape as a variety of new social practices emerged around the sharing of texts, forms that brought together new groups of people in new ways. The Parisian salon was one of the most famous examples, where learned wit was combined with the circulation of letters, poems, and the day's newest philosophy, all under the tutelage of a powerful matriarch or *salonnière*, like Marie Thérèse Geoffrin in Paris or Rahel Varnhagen in Berlin.

The London coffeehouse was another such place. As a French observer remarked, "To improve Society, the English have, besides their usual and friendly Meetings called *Clubs*, the Conveniency of *Coffee-Houses*, more common here than anywhere else. In which all Corners intermix together, with mutual freedom; and, at a very easy Rate Men have the Opportunity of meeting together, and getting Acquaintance, with choice of Conversation, besides the Advantage of reading all foreign and domestic News."[13] Unlike the stylishness of the Parisian or Viennese café, the London coffeehouse was imagined to be a place of social and textual commonality.

Common reading spaces were a hallmark of the urbanizing cultures of eighteenth-century Europe, as the rising accessibility of reading helped further disseminate Enlightenment ideals of humanity, equality, and general learning. In Edinburgh in 1720, a group of women came together every week under the heading of the Fair Intellectual Club to discuss books and promote "Female Excellence."[14] It was the first of many subsequent examples of the way men and women would convene to decide on what to read. "We cannot be too careful in the Choice of Authors and Subjects," wrote the fair intellectuals in their public manifesto. In the German territories close to fifty reading clubs were founded in the first half of the eighteenth century. Over the next two decades 370 more were established. "Every friend of literature can become a member of the society," read the first article of the "constitution" of one such society in Bonn.[15] Rises in literacy did not initially imply a world of isolated readers devouring material

[FIGURE 5.3] One can see from this popular depiction of the social circle surrounding the Duchess Anna Amalia in Weimar the variety of things people did together while gathered around a table. Reading is only one activity among many. Georg Melchior Kraus, *Evening Company with Anna Amalia* (1795). Courtesy of the Klassik Stiftung Weimar, Goethe-Nationalmuseum.

alone in their bedrooms or boudoirs. Instead, it signaled the way individuals increasingly lived in a world where reading was an ever greater part of social life (fig. 5.3).

The book's growing prominence within the eighteenth century and its democratizing impulses were no historical accident. The book was, and continues to be, thought of as an important medium of democratization. But with every new social habit of promoting access to reading came a subsidiary one of keeping other readers out. Coffeehouses and royal societies were for men only, Fair Intellectual Clubs by definition for the fair sex, salons only for the most fashionable, and reading clubs were far more exclusive than their "constitutions" let on, accompanied as they were by membership fees and strict rules of dress. Open circles of sentimental readers in the eighteenth century gradually gave way to cults of nationalistic brotherhood in the nineteenth. The book's availability transformed into fears of reading madness and maladies like bibliomania. As Emerson himself acknowledged in his essay on friendship, "Friendship, like the immortality of the soul, is too good to be believed."

When the famed eighteenth-century protagonists of Goethe's *The Sorrows of Young Werther* begin to passionately discuss the new novels of their day, they only belatedly notice that they have left everyone else out of the conversation. Our attachments to reading, and our desire to share them, can wittingly or unwittingly be the tools through which we push others away, including those with whom we have tried to share. Reading divides as much as it brings us together. No matter how much books have been shared throughout time, at least part of the history of reading is a record of miscomprehension and misjudgment. This is reading's edge.

There is no more poignant scene of this problem than in Virginia Woolf's *To the Lighthouse* (1927), one of the great novels about reading. One evening, after the children have gone to bed, Mr. and Mrs. Ramsay are reading together. He is reading Walter Scott and Honoré de Balzac, "the English novel and the French novel." She is reading Shakespeare's sonnets. Unlike her husband, she does not read genres, but line by line. "'Nor praise the deep vermilion rose,'" she reads, quoting Shakespeare's ninety-eighth sonnet to herself. "How satisfying! How restful!" she thinks. "All the odds and ends of the day stuck to this magnet." For Mrs. Ramsay, the sonnet captured the "essence sucked out of life and held rounded here." It was a beautiful sentiment about the way certain words can make perfect sense of the otherwise jumbled nature of our daily lives. In the company of another, however, such bliss can be short-lived.

> But she was becoming conscious of her husband looking at her. He was smiling at her, quizzically, as if he were ridiculing her gently for being asleep in broad daylight, but at the same time he was

thinking, Go on reading. You don't look sad now, he thought. And he wondered what she was reading, and exaggerated her ignorance, her simplicity, for he liked to think that she was not clever, not book-learned at all. He wondered if she understood what she was reading. Probably not, he thought.

"Well?" she said, echoing his smile dreamily, looking up from her book.[16]

"Probably not" is one of the most piercing lines I have ever read. He cannot know how deeply, how "well" she *has* understood Shakespeare, how meaningful that moment of reading has been for her. It has made her well, and yet she cannot share it with him ("Well?" she says). How could they ever have this experience in common? A chasm exists between husband and wife and reading only deepens it. Reading is a sign of what cannot be shared between two people. His words reveal a profound truth in their condescension.

In the letters of the twentieth-century poets Paul Celan and Ingeborg Bachmann we find a moving, real-world equivalent of Woolf's predicament. Celan and Bachmann, who had a brief love affair after the Second World War, were two of the most important postwar writers to work in the German language, she an Austrian woman contending with what it meant to write for a male-dominated literary market, he a Romanian Jew contending with what it meant to write after the Holocaust. Few writers have had a more intense relationship with the nature of language. In their letters we can see how they are like opposing poles of a magnet, so similar, and yet so irreconcilable.

Celan was living in Paris, while Bachmann was in Vienna. Their correspondence, irregular from the start (like their affair), is supported by moments of sharing their writing with one another. After their second affair in 1957, she sends him her radio play *The Good God of Manhattan*, and he replies by sending her some of Rimbaud's poetry. A few months later he will send his new collection of poems *Speech-Grille*. Their letters are delicate balancing acts, with requests to see each other and replies of deferral. They are concerned with what cannot be said and what will inevitably not be understood. "You know, Ingeborg, yes you know," writes Celan. "And us," she writes, "oh Paul, you know." "You know," they write repeatedly, because, as Bachmann later suggests, "I don't know the word that could completely capture what sustains us."[17]

A break happens in 1959 when Celan receives a scathing and overtly anti-Semitic review of his new poetry collection. Bachmann writes to console him, but he is deeply hurt by what he sees as her misunderstanding of the stakes of his writing. This isn't about style, he says, it's about the memory of my mother's death in a concentration camp. He asks her never to write to him again. For Bachmann, years of frustration at the one-sidedness of their conversation well up as she replies, "I will hear you, but you must help me by hearing me too." A few months later she writes, "For us there can be nothing further." Nevertheless, they continue to exchange letters—and books. He sends her poems by Paul Valéry, she sends Gertrude Stein in return. He sends more of his own poems, she sends her collection of stories *The Thirtieth Year* (1961). Finally, though, the letters break off. Nine years later in April 1970, Celan will throw himself in the Seine. Three years later Bachmann will die from burns after passing out in her bed with a lit cigarette.

Two of the greatest writers of the twentieth century sustained a friendship through sharing reading. And yet sharing persistently drew attention to the way they were always writing, and reading, past one another. If you look closely at their letters, a book is most often shared at those moments when something has been misunderstood. The closer we are, whether physically or intellectually, the less we need to share. Sharing is a sign of shearing, a fork in the road to which we cannot return.

+ +

On October 15, 1973, six months after I was born, Ken Thompson of Bell Labs delivered a talk on what was then the third version of the Unix operating system. He spoke before a small audience at the Association for Computing Machinery's Annual Symposium on Operating Systems Principles that was taking place at the IBM Watson Research Center in Yorktown Heights, New York. The publication of the talk a year later marked a decisive turning point in the fortunes of Unix and the development of operating systems. Requests flooded in for copies of the software, which were then shared on RKo5 disks or nine-track tapes. In a virtual feedback loop, the more people that had access to Unix, the more people were trained on it, the more they contributed to its further development. Unix would subsequently become the single most important operating system in the development of computing, forming the backbone of the emerging Arpanet and every major corporate operating system from Windows to Sun to Apple.

Unix's success, and eventual eclipse, was critically related to the problem of sharing. In a very basic sense, sharing is what an operating system does: it makes decisions about sharing the processing resources of a machine (Unix was formally known as "The Unix Time Sharing System"). Prior to operating systems, scientists used sign-up sheets to share large mainframe computers that could only run one program at a time.[18] The early computer lab was akin to the medieval monastery with its scarcity of copies. The operating system took the idea of shared access to a scarce resource and implemented it at the internal level of the machine.

But sharing was integral to the development of Unix in another way as well. One of the keys to Unix's success was not just its simplicity and elegance (something programmers repeatedly highlighted). It was also the weak licensing culture to which it belonged. Because Bell Labs was partially owned by AT&T, and because AT&T at the time was a state-regulated monopoly, it was forbidden from entering subsidiary markets. It therefore took a rather aloof role in licensing the operating system, allowing its source code to be shared for a nominal price (something unimaginable today). It was this historical accident that resulted in Unix's initial availability among the computer science community and that in turn led to its development. As Peter Salus writes, "The decision on the part of the AT&T lawyers to allow educational institutions to receive Unix, but to deny support or bug fixes had an immediate effect: it forced the users to share with one another. They shared ideas, information, programs, bug fixes, and hardware fixes."[19] That sharedness resulted in the spread, adoption, and adaptation of Unix into hundreds of different forms (fig. 5.4).

It was this sharedness, when coupled with the opposing trend toward the rising proprietization of code, that led to Unix's de-

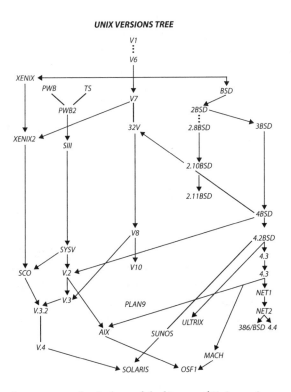

[FIGURE 5.4] A chart of the history of Unix versions, adapted from Peter H. Salus, *A Quarter Century of Unix* (Reading, MA: Addison-Wesley, 1994), 61.

mise as an industry standard. The more it was shared, the more it bifurcated into different versions, versions that eventually came to compete with one another. The original became Unix System V owned by AT&T. Berkeley Unix became BSD, Free BSD, 386BSD, NetBSD, and OpenBSD, as well as the basis of Sun Microsystems's Solaris. Andrew Tanenbaum created Minix, which then turned into Linux, one of the great stories of open-source computing. Sharing was not just a force of commonality. It was a powerful tool for generating a landscape of prodigious versional diversity.

The history of computing, like the history of books, is related at a deep level to a culture of sharing. Unix was no different. From the rise of the free software movement to its rival idea of open-source software, from the rise of time-sharing operating systems to information networks, from the Whole Earth Catalogue to new-wave theories of the coming Singularity, computer program-ming has been suffused with ideals of sharing and sharedness from its inception, in both theory and practice.[20] When we lament the oversharing of social media today we do well to remember these communal roots of digital culture. But we would do just as well to remember the particular story of Unix, the law of forking that stands behind it.

Sharing is now a default setting on almost all digital reading in-terfaces. The question is no longer if you would like to share what you are reading but how. As the sociologist Antoine Hennion has argued, such networks of amateur interest—or "taste" from Hen-nion's French perspective—facilitate greater self-reflection on the part of readers. Like the amateur wine drinker who looks up from his glass to explain his thoughts rather than just consume the wine, when we choose to share our reading with someone else we are engaging in a moment of self-reflection, a "perplexed state," in Hennion's words. But we are also testing our relationship to ideas against those around us. "Taste," writes Hennion, "lived by each but fashioned by all, is a history of oneself permanently remade together with others."[21]

We not only share as readers, but we are also increasingly

encouraged to do so as writers. "Collaboration" is the new watch-word of the day. From Thomas Carlyle's nineteenth-century homage to individualism *On Heroes and Hero Worship* (1841), we have moved to online tools like Brain Candy, where readers are reconceived as "content producers in their own right" who participate in the "co-creation of value." Teen writing sites, cell-phone novels, and now the holy grail of publishing, the app, are all forums where readers' comments can be incorporated into this latest version of serialized writing. Long live the Victorian novel.

These tools, and many more like them, are manifestations of Henry Jenkins's notion of participatory culture, where fans coproduce the world of content that belongs to an artistic work. For Jenkins such practices are part and parcel of the realization of a new collective intelligence: "None of us can know everything; each of us knows something; and we can put the pieces together if we pool our resources and combine our skills."[22] Where we used to think in binary terms of production and consumption or read-ing and writing, theorists today speak of things like "produsage" (production through use) and "wreading" (where every time you read a digital text you generate, or write, a unique version of it).[23] Wikipedia is the god of this new order of neologisms.

And right on cue we find a host of new "anti-social manifes-toes" and appeals for more rugged individualism.[24] We continue to worry about oversharing. But in many ways, this just takes us back to the origins of writing, which was thought to be a gift of the gods. Whether it belonged to the muse, a holy spirit, or the vox populi, our reading material has most often been imagined to belong to something greater than ourselves. "Knowledge is a gift of God, therefore it cannot be sold," went a common me-dieval saying.[25] As a variety of critics have pointed out, there are profound ethical implications of thinking about reading in this way. You don't have to believe in Raymond Kurzweil's no-tion of "The Singularity"—the moment when humans will tran-scend their biological foundations and exist as one networked consciousness online—to feel the pronounced sense of how we are being woven together today through our digital reading.[26] The question remains whether such collective work could ever produce something more creative than a committee report or an encyclopedia. *The Runes of Gallidon*—Brain Candy's first collaborative work—is no *Aeneid*.

Such collective fantasies have a long and venerable past, by no means alien to the world of books and print. The editors of the early nineteenth-century periodical the *Athenaeum* similarly dreamed of "the combination of individual thought into one mighty mass of intellect, that vast embodied essence of society called Public Opinion."[27] The newspaper was to be the medium of the universal mind.

The recurrence of such fantasies would be all well and good if it were not for two troubling facts. The first is what we might call the problem of the "nondisplay view," the use of data by corporations or governments that is not tied to the immediate presentation of that data. When distributors of electronic books store your reading data or annotations on their servers; when search engines store your page views; when social networking sites store everything you write, you are by default sharing your reading, whether you want to or not. It may not be "public" (i.e., on display), but it is being read. In this scenario you're not an amateur or connoisseur, one who loves or knows, but a test subject, someone who is constantly being measured. The fantasy of the circle of readers—whether it was in the woods, the coffeehouse, or the living room—was the way it put you outside of *some other circle*. It was fashioned as a means of escape (from life, work, the public sphere, or an evil aunt). Sharing and privacy may be rhetorically opposed today, but they are historically linked. The return of the "pirate bay" is one example of a digital space where readers are still attempting to share privately with one another or control when they share.

The second problem takes the rather inelegant form of "the license." If there is a Singularity out there, it is copyright law. Not only are ever more facets of intellectual life thought to be copyrightable—up to and including life itself—but the restrictions surrounding what others can do with such material are becoming increasingly extensive. When early modern printers received a royal license (a *privilège* in French), it restricted other people's right to print books. But it said nothing about what readers could do. In the new licensing culture, it is readers who are now granted a license, because everyone is potentially a printer. We no longer buy books, we borrow them. The dream of the universal library has turned into the library as the universal way of accessing books—with mandatory fees. We don't purchase, we agree to terms of use (all the time). This is incidentally how children interact with objects, always conditionally. We are either absolute borrowers or absolute owners. We have lost mechanisms through which we hand something over to another, through which readers make something *their own*.

In 2001, a group of intellectual property experts and computer scientists founded the Creative Commons. It is to the culture industry what the Free Software Foundation is to computing. It creates, distributes, and supports licenses that are more nuanced than the "all rights reserved" logic of copyright. With a Creative Commons license you can allow people to download and share your material for free or even rework it for their own commercial gain. The movement's goal is to restore a certain reasonableness to digital practices of sharing, to reclaim habits and practices that were once "common" but that have increasingly become criminalized under the new licensing regime. The larger aim is the creation of a legal "space" that is immune to the reach of copyright, a domain where we can borrow, remix, and share ideas with minimal limitations.

As James Boyle, one of the group's founders, has argued, Creative Commons is modeled on the environmental movement of the 1960s.[28] Like the "environment," there is an abstraction out there called the public domain (now the intellectual commons) that is diminishing and that our laws are encouraging us to diminish. By giving this space a name and publicizing the irrationality of our incursions, the hope is to motivate us to change our ways. Or rather, for some of us to change our ways so that others do not have to. The beauty of the environmental movement was that, like the environment, it required a total effort. Everyone was affected—consumers and producers alike had to make sacrifices to restore elementary things like water, air, and the earth back to health. The problem with the Creative Commons is that it makes no claims on how consumers (formerly readers) think about the practices of sharing it intends to protect.

For some, the combination of technological change and new political infrastructures like Creative Commons or the Free Software Foundation could begin to significantly alter our relationship to intellectual property for the first time since its institutionalization in the eighteenth century.[29] In this view, the last two hundred years might one day be seen as a brief, and aberrant, period, like when we believed in ghosts (i.e., intellectual property). For others, we are witnessing nothing more than a new gilded age of the proprietization of thought for the few at the expense of the many.[30]

What both positions overlook is the way sharing and owning have historically been related to one another. Sharing and owning are not the agons we typically make them out to be, but two aspects within a larger spectrum of how we relate to ideas. All systems of intellectual property, even the most collective, have had some form of personal ownership, of how we internalize the ideas of a community and make them our own, just as all forms of commercial property exist alongside robust economies of sharing. The periodic rise of invocations of "friendship" surrounding reading, whether in the form of Renaissance humanism or American transcendentalism, *Alba amicorum* or Gift Books, are nothing more than the cyclical correctives to the rising commercialization of reading during these same periods. Along with luminaries such as Erasmus or Emerson, numerous individuals were attempting to work out new ways and new technologies of holding reading in common, while also acknowledging the limits that such commonality posed.

We are at a similar moment today. At issue is not the owning or disowning of ideas, free culture versus commodity culture.

Rather, at issue is their proper integration, how we can move from the one *to* the other. At issue is how we can share *well*. When we use terms like "Creative Commons," "wiki," or even "Brain Candy," we are making assumptions about the inherent commonality of ideas—that they are "as common as air" in Judge Brandeis's formulation in one of the foundational cases of intellectual property law, requiring no more work than breathing in to absorb them.

And yet there is nothing inherently common about the intellectual commons.[31] The history of sharing books, as well as software, tells a different story. Remember Unix and the law of forking. "Free" is useless for figuring out a system of value, meaning, and commonality. It just creates the proliferation of multiple, usually incompatible, versions. This is the tragedy of the intellectual commons—not overuse, but what amounts to its opposite: overproliferation. Sharing, and sharing well, is what brings that proliferation into a meaningful order. Licensing culture is by itself not enough.

If we are going to do something transformative about the problem of intellectual property, we must attend more to the practices of sharing and not just the laws and the technologies that constrain it. In this, the history of books can once more be instructive. As we saw with Celan and Bachmann, real sharing takes time. There is an asynchrony to sharing that cannot be speeded up. *Wiki*, the Hawaiian word for "fast," belies the time it takes to have ideas in common. We need to design more for time in our so-called social media.

But we also need to design more for scarcity. Copying is not the same as sharing. Having a file in common that we can both access at the same time overlooks any sense of personal investment in the process, that which makes sharedness possible. In order to share something, I must also give something up. This is the lesson of childhood, Adam's rib, and the history of book givers like Mauranus, Aldrovandi, and Shakespeare. To this end, we need— brace yourself for this—to embrace DRM. Instead of making it a crime to share, we should be making it easier to share when it is conditioned upon loss. Just as when I give a material object to someone, we should be able to transfer rights more easily from one person to another. Only then will the two of us feel what it means to impart and part with something as the beginning of our mutual understanding.

Making digital objects more unique, and thus less copyable, also means making them easier to interact with, to do more things to and with them. The problem with DRM is not that it tries to make digital objects more like print objects. The problem is that in doing so it loses many of the personalizing features that belonged to books. Marginalia, dedications, rebinding, putting things into books—these were all ways that one could make a copy unique and thus more meaningful when one gave it away. As the Victorian essayist Leigh Hunt remarked, "One precious name, or little inscription at the beginning of the volume . . . is worth all the binding in St. James's."[32] We need a more layered notion of DRM, one that can guarantee the uniqueness of an object as well as our ability to interact with it. Only in this way can we make it our own and thus give something of ourselves away when we share it.

If genuine sharing involves a certain element of sacrifice, of giving something up, it also entails an acknowledgment of limits. Not everything can be shared. This is the lesson of the fable of St. Martin who cut his coat in half to give to a beggar. If we shared everything, we would have nothing left to share. Oversharing only exists as a problem if we spend too little time cultivating something our own. What I do not share or cannot share is truly who I am. More time thinking about and designing for our un-shareables, all those aspects of our mental and emotional lives that are inalienable, will serve as an important antidote to the perceived oversharing of social media today. As the contemporary artist Aram Bartholl has shown, it means imagining more of what he calls "dead drops," spaces where information does not go anywhere, in this case memory sticks imbedded in the walls of cities throughout the world (fig. 5.5). Bartholl's work is a moving

[FIGURE 5.5]   Aram Bartholl, *Dead Drops*
(2010). Courtesy of the artist.

digital version of the ancient practice of whispering secrets into the hollows of trees.

Finally, genuine sharing is about taking care of something not your own once it has been given to you. Being shared with comes with an obligation. Unlike a gift, you are more of a custodian than an owner of a shared object. In creative terms, it would be the difference between the novels of someone like the German émigré writer W. G. Sebald, who meticulously records the stories of Jewish emigrants and their memories after the war using a complicated web of indirect discourse, and the many digital forms of the "remix" or "mash-up" today. In Sebald, someone else's story becomes interwoven into his own, but it still remains partially intact, never entirely his. *Mashing*, as the name viscerally tells us, lacks this sense of care or responsibility for something or someone else. It eschews commonality in the name of the commons.

I realize that criticizing remix culture and embracing DRM puts me on the wrong side of history (how old is this guy anyway?). But despite the grand claims of "everything is social" today, there is remarkably little mutuality online. On the one hand, the history of books tells us this is as it should be—having ideas in common is extremely difficult. But the history of books also gives us a glimpse into a variety of practices that can help mitigate the shearing of reading, the way it divides us as much as it brings us together. Instead of more antisocial manifestoes or more paeans to free culture, we need greater attention to the contradictions inherent in what Emerson defined as true intellectual friendship: "We will meet as though we met not, and part as though we parted not."[33]

+ +

At the opening of his evocative essay on unpacking his library, Walter Benjamin suggested that one of the best ways to build a library of one's own is through inheritance.[34] I often think about this when I look at my own library. Modest as it is (I am no book collector), will my children want all of these books when I am dead? What if they don't read German, or if they find that there are too few in French, or if they just don't want *books* anymore? Will my library be referred to, as was the case in one probate inventory from the seventeenth century, as "his books and other trash"?[35]

Whether personal or institutional, a library is a space of sharing. Books share space with other books, accruing value through their proximity. The "stack" or "pile" is one of the most fundamental ways that books have meaning for us. But in placing books on a shelf, owners are also sharing books with others. Look, says a bookshelf, here is a collection of my ideas.

A hard drive, on the other hand, is a curious kind of library. Instead of books, it is full of files, which are not stacked, but imbedded within one another. The hard drive is more like a law office. Depending on whom those files "belong" to, they can or cannot be shared with others. But unlike books on the bookshelf, files on hard drives cannot be visually shared with those around us (or even with ourselves—files nested within each other do not allow for an easy visual sense of the whole). Hard drives do not perform in quite the same way as shelves.

Perhaps in response, more and more of our collecting is happening in the clouds. Like Cory Arcangel's *Super Mario Clouds* (2002), which reworked the popular video game so that viewers only saw the clouds floating in the background, clouds are where we dream of the collectivity of ideas.[36] New websites like Public Collectors are helping make our digital collections available and shareable online. Unlike the bounded nature of our studies, homes, books, or even hard drives, cloud collections are more interchangeable. As Mimi Zeiger has written, today we no longer collect objects, we collect collections.[37] We share presentations of our own and other people's digital "shelves" without possessing anything tangible underneath, indeed without a strong sense of possession. The inherent tension of any collection—between having and halving, between owning and transmitting—is now decidedly tilted in the direction of commonality.

But if I do not have my collection of digital files in the same way as my books, will I be able to give them away in the same manner? When I pass down my books to my children, I imagine I will be sharing with them a sense of time. Books are meaningful because as material objects they bear time within themselves. They convey a sense of time passing in a double sense—my having been there for some period of time and my no longer being there ("I was there," a book says). Digital files, on the other hand, do not register time in quite this way. In order for them to remain legible to both machines and humans, they must be continually translated into new formats ("migrated" in technical terms). Files overwrite time. My physical copy of Ralph Ellison's *Invisible Man*, with its signature Vintage cover, its now slightly faded pages, its dog-ears, and its occasional uneven underlinings, will tell my children something that my digital copy of George Sand's *Indiana* will not. We may look at a machine and feel a sense of time (my Apple IIe if I had kept it), but we cannot, currently at least, look at a file and feel time in the same way.

And yet when I share my books with my children, I will only be sharing a part of me. There is only so much my children will ever learn about me. Even less so from my library. As they hold my books in their hands, they will be holding on to something that I once held. They will be able to look at my annotations, which are usually underlinings, but also occasionally notes in the margins summarizing what I've read or even less frequently ideas in the back pages for books or essays that I would like to write in the future. They will also be able to see where I gave up when I was reading, where the pages begin to look suspiciously unused.

But through it all they will experience how little of me, how little of what I was doing during all those hours when I was reading, can be communicated to them. Unlike the digital file, which exists in a far more exacting web of measurability (when I read it, how long I read it, what I did with it), the used book is remarkably unmarked by comparison. In passing down my books I am passing down a sense of aloneness, of dwelling in myself. I am passing down a sense of difference. When I share my books with my children, I will be sharing the limits of sharing. Books are the original difference engines.

SIX

Among the Trees

And this our life, exempt from public haunt,
Finds tongues in trees, books in the running brooks,
Sermons in stones, and good in every thing.

WILLIAM SHAKESPEARE [*as you like it*]

On a moonlit evening in 1772 in a wooded grove outside of Göttingen, seven young men gathered together to pledge their allegiance to poetry and each other. They crowned their hats with leaves, placed them beneath a large oak tree, and began to dance in a circle around the tree while holding hands. As one member later wrote to a friend, they called upon the moon and the stars to be their witnesses to this new *Bund* or union. They read poems aloud and pledged to do so at regular weekly meetings. One week later they met again and began recording their poetry in a book. It was inscribed with the words "The Union is Eternal." And so was born one of the most influential poetic movements of the eighteenth century that came to be known as the Union of the Göttingen Grove.[1]

By the end of the eighteenth century reading outdoors was decidedly in vogue. As the last chains on books were being removed from libraries, men and women were going out into the woods to read books more than ever before. They were in search of peace and quiet, but also communion—with nature and with one another (fig. 6.1). Reading outdoors brought readers together

[FIGURE 6.1] Heinrich Beck, *Five Women Reading Werther* (n.d.). Courtesy of the Goethe-Museum Düsseldorf, Germany.

through the naturalness of their feelings, not the artificial constraints of the salon or the schoolroom. Like the sinewy and subterranean connections of the trees' roots, outdoor reading was a way to feel more intertwined with one another through the shared caverns of inner sentiment. Outdoor reading made readers feel more connected.

If the vogue for reading in the woods brought readers together in new ways, it also brought readers and their books together in new ways as well. Reading among the trees was a means of connecting with a sense of the book's origins at a time when books were appearing in ever greater numbers. Both the English "book" and German *Buch* derive from the word for beech tree, while in India, it was the birch tree that served as one of the first writing surfaces. The Latin *codex*, which is the technical term used for books, derives from the word for the trunk of a tree. And the Greek *biblion*, from which we have both "Bible" and "bibliography," comes from the name of the Phoenician town

Byblus, which was a major exporter of papyrus, the plant that served as a key early writing surface for books in the Mediterranean region and beyond.

Reading among the trees was thus a literal reminder of where books came from. As in the medieval tree of knowledge or Darwin's tree of descent, reading among the trees—reading understood *as* a tree—was a quest for origins (fig. 6.2). It was a way of reading backward, a search for roots. But in those seemingly endless forking paths of the trees' branches, readers also began

[FIGURE 6.2]   Ramon Llull, *Arbor Scientiae* (1505), SC.L9665.482ab.
Courtesy of Houghton Library, Harvard University.

to see a potent symbol for the branching of readerly thought, what the poet John Keats memorably called "the mazy world of silvery enchantment."[2] In turning outward toward the woods, the tree reminded readers of a turn inward into the expanse of human thought. Even at its most experientially poignant (being in nature), reading a book outdoors could serve as a means of accessing no place at all. It served as a space to lose one's sense of place.

Reading in the woods is just one example of the way reading is deeply shaped by where we read. Whether on trains, planes, buses, in bed, at a carrel, by a bookshelf, or under a tree, we will read just about anywhere. But as Gertrude Stein understood in those words, "book was there," it matters deeply *where* one reads. Reading and place conjoin to form a powerful mix of meaning. "Oh what I would have given to be able to read my Homer on board," wrote the young German pastor Johann Gottfried Herder in 1769 as he made his way at the beginning of his career from Europe's outskirts in Riga to the continent's intellectual center. Every book has its place.

Today, the space of reading seems increasingly unsettled. Digital technologies are premised on a core conviction, almost religious in tone, about the power of mobility. Reading is once again on the move. At the same time, reading is in more places and more versions than ever before. We live in what is called a multiscreen reality.[3] Where early cinemagoers were struck by the imposing size of the projected image, its monumental singularity, our interactions with screens are increasingly broken up into different spaces, formats, and versions. Diminution is followed by dissemination. This too has important bibliographic precedents. Where the large-format *folio* was the premier textual instrument of the Renaissance, the growing commercialization of reading in the nineteenth century led to more differentiated types of books to be read in more diverse settings (schools, bedrooms, trains, etc).

But where the book was both somewhere and nowhere—the way its strongly place-bound nature allowed readers to lose a sense of place while reading—digital texts by contrast are almost always somewhere and *elsewhere*. Woven ever more tightly into our daily lives, digital texts are more intensely place bound than books ever were. The ubiquity of cell phones, GPS devices, radio frequency ID tags, and new location services like Foursquare ("unlock your city") mean that our texts are not only with us wherever we go, they are there to keep us from getting lost. And yet in their highly distributed nature, they are broken up across new, and increasingly transnational, geographies. What does it mean for a reader to be in so many places at once?

The history of reading is indebted to the spaces where we read and the types of reading these spaces promote. But our reading *tools* have also played an important role in establishing a connection between individuals and a sense of place. Reading material isn't just there. It helps structure our relationship to space and thus the space of thought.

+ +

Reading has for much of its history been associated with a sense of intimacy. We not only hold books before us in a sense of prayer, we also cradle them. Augustine's conversion, we remember, took place in response to the child's voice singing the refrain, "Take it and read." Well before the invention of childhood reading, the book spoke to us in the familiar sounds of the lullaby.

When we look at images of readers, we very often find them in corners (fig. 6.3).[4] As Gaston Bachelard writes of the corner, "An imaginary room rises up around our bodies. The shadows are walls, a piece of furniture is a barrier, hangings are a roof."[5] The corner is both an inside and an outside. It folds back on us, a space within a space. The Gothic cathedrals of European monasteries abounded with corners, which were used by monks as reading spaces. As reading moved out of the study and into the home, people began to speak of the reading nook. This is where we "curl up" with a (or the) "good book." The book's goodness is a function of its power of enclosure. The Romantic bower, that

[FIGURE 6.3]   Headpiece from Leigh Hunt, *A Book for a Corner*
(1849). Courtesy of Victoria University Library, Toronto.

dreamy space of enchantment and "curtain'd canopies" (again
Keats), was another way of imagining this inside without.

In the corner we make ourselves smaller, curling, coiling, and
contracting. It is where we dream of the miniature. The miniature
book, defined as being less than three inches on a side and dating
back to the fifteenth century, belongs to this space of the recess,
to a time out.[6] Thumb Bibles, finger calendars, or the Mignon
Almanacs of publishers like Joseph Riedl in Vienna—these were
all popular ways that reading shrank over the centuries, as in
Jones & Company's *Traveling Library* (1824–32), which contained fifty-three volumes of British classics in a single case that
measured nine by seventeen inches. When opened, it resembled a

classical Greek temple. Small books were the physical expressions of small characters, some of the most popular in the history of literature, like Tom Thumb, the Lilliputians, or Goethe's Melusina, a nymph who lived in a traveling (book) case.

The miniature contracts time and space, but it does so to expand them in a different register. "Miniature is one of the refuges of greatness," says Bachelard.[7] It is a foretaste of something to come, a reminder of the strong connection between intimacy and "intimation." In this way, the miniature world of the nook, bower, or garden is a space of utopia (literally meaning no place). But it is also one of folly. Like so many characters from W. G. Sebald's fictions who work on small, irrelevant things, the miniature can be useless, mundane, even self-destructive.[8] As Toni Morrison writes in *Paradise*, "How exquisitely human was the wish for permanent happiness, and how thin human imagination became trying to achieve it."[9] The miniature is how we live with the extraordinary, with overly grand ideas like "paradise." The nook may open out into an imaginative expanse, like the windows that were above medieval reading desks for a lack of interior lighting or the streams that were compulsory for the bower's architecture. But the nook also allows us to reenter the world—to go back to work.

Reading in the corner or beneath a tree is a way of taking time. It takes time away from something, but it also has a duration. That is why debates about reading can be so contested today—it sits uncomfortably within the iron laws of productivity. The gods of efficiency look disapprovingly upon readers. The increasingly fragile state of the humanities has much to do with the fact that it is a field largely premised on reading a great deal.[10]

In order to take the time to read, individuals need support, and not just the institutional kind. Reading can also be physically tiring. It seems to run counter to the body's natural rhythms. As the book historian Erich Schön has pointed out, there is a rich tradition of reading imagery in which we see readers resting their heads on their hands while they read (fig. 6.4).[11] The history of

[FIGURE 6.4] Adolf Schroedter, *Don Quixote Sitting in an Armchair While Reading the Chivalric Novel "Amadis of Gaul"* (1834). Courtesy of bpk Berlin/Nationalgalerie, Staatliche Museen, Berlin, Germany. Photo: Klaus Goeken/Art Resource, New York.

reading is as much about furniture as it is architecture and economics, the places where we rest our heads or our backs at the same time that we hold our books aloft.

With the spread of consumer culture at the end of the eighteenth century, new specialized reading chairs were invented for the home, places where individuals could forget about their bodies as they read (fig. 6.5). As Edgar Allen Poe would write in his "Philosophy of Furniture," describing his ideal domestic décor, "Repose speaks in all."[12] The book, and the material support to

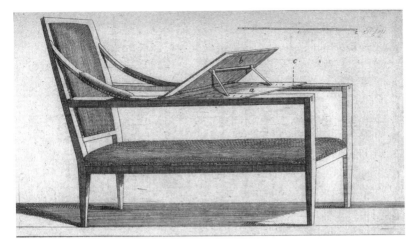

[FIGURE 6.5] Reading chair from the *Journal des Luxus und der Moden* (February 1799). Courtesy of the Klassik Stiftung Weimar, HAAB/ZA-2011.

which it corresponded, was understood as a form of rest—it allowed readers to rest from the rigors of daily life; to rest on it in the sense of depending on something; and finally it was a form of rest in the sense of waste, of something leftover (as in what are you going to do with the rest of that?). The book was there so that we wouldn't have to be.

Reading among the trees was gradually complemented by another kind of outdoor reading, that of reading in the streets, which had much to do with the rise of metropolitan centers in Europe and North America in the nineteenth and twentieth centuries. Like its pastoral counterpart, the urban landscape was imagined to abound with corners—the edge of a park bench, a seat in the subway, a bus stop, a stairwell, a stoop, a sculpture, an overhang, or an underpass. But unlike the domestic cranny or the idyllic bower, the meaning of the urban recess was darker, more menacing. It was a gateway to uncertainty, updating the threatening aspects of the fairy tale set in the woods (a space both open and closed, but always too large). Speaking of Paris in the mid-nineteenth century, Baudelaire would write of the "sinuous folds of the old capital," while Thomas de Quincey would muse on the "knotty problems of alleys" and the "enigmatical entries" of London's streets during his opium-laden wanderings in the 1820s.[13]

For the twentieth-century philosopher and journalist Siegfried Kracauer, who recorded his walks through the seedier pockets of Berlin between the world wars, the city was populated by an urban underclass for whom "nothing was any longer at-hand."[14] Unlike the naturalist in the woods or the comfortable home-dwellers who were losing themselves in their books, in the hollow city of modern life readers were increasingly getting lost. It was out of these urban recesses that emerged new experimental forms of writing, from the Dada headquarters of the Cabaret Voltaire in Zurich in 1916 to CBGB in 1970s New York, which helped spawn the punk "zine."[15] The urban nook, social resistance, and the reimagined page went hand in hand.

Books not only help us get lost—whether in ourselves or in the world—they also help us find our way. The travel guide dates back to the popular genre of the *Ars apodemica*, a dense compendium of information about foreign spaces that owed much to the encyclopedic urges of the Renaissance.[16] It came into its own in the nineteenth century with the rise of tourism, supported through popular travel series from publishers like Karl Baedeker in Germany or John Murray in Britain. These books taught us where to go and what to see. Goethe said that having a travel guide in Italy was like watching a book lying on embers—it gradually shriveled up in the face of the real thing.[17] But he would also spend his evenings revisiting the books of buildings or plants he had seen during the day. The book has an oscillatory relationship to travel, opening and closing to reveal something deeper about where we are.

Nowhere is this oscillation of reading more important than when we don't go very far: when we browse. The term "browsing" comes from the now obsolete noun "browse," for the young shoots of a tree. Although it was only used in relation to reading

[FIGURE 6.6]   Book wheel from Agostino Ramelli,
Le diverse et artificiose machine (1588). Courtesy of the
Elizabethan Club of Yale University, New Haven, CT.

for the first time in the nineteenth century, the practice is far older. Take, for example, the famed scholar's wheel, as imagined by the Renaissance engineer Agostino Ramelli (fig. 6.6). The serenity of the book's single, turned page is transformed into the heavy, *churning* revolutions of the book wheel (recalling no doubt that proto-industrial processor, the mill wheel). Sometimes one book will simply not do. When we read we often triangulate multiple sources to arrive at the truth.[18]

By the twentieth century, churning had acquired the sense of churning out, to produce something of lesser quality. Surplus has become decidedly negative, but not so for earlier readers. We may dream in the nook, but we also need places where we can skip, skim, churn, graze, browse, or process. As Emerson remarked, "Often a chapter is enough. The glance reveals when the gaze obscures."[19] Discontinuous reading was and still is one of the most important types of reading. As Roland Barthes remarks, "We read a text (of pleasure) the way a fly buzzes around a room: with sudden, deceptively decisive turns, fervent and futile."[20]

If the book wheel called upon a certain kind of athletic reading (like the fervent fly), it was the invention of the bookshelf that projected a more patient as well as optical relationship to reading—of seeing, but also being seen. As Henry Petroski has pointed out in his marvelous history of the bookshelf, bookshelves did not always look the way they do today, and books were not always stacked vertically next to one another with their spines out.[21] But as the bookshelf gradually developed into its modern form, strolling through the "stacks" of libraries or bookstores was often seen as a way of being fashionable. The setting of all those elegantly bound books in nice cases cast a flattering light on one's own sense of personal encasement.

As readers strolled by bookshelves looking at each other, they were no doubt also making mental images of the books that were passing by. They were reading the place of books. As Sartre writes of browsing through his grandfather's study as a young boy, "Though I did not yet know how to read, I already revered those standing stones: upright or leaning over, close together like bricks on the book-shelves or spaced out nobly in lanes of menhirs. They all looked alike. I disported myself in a tiny sanctuary, surrounded by ancient, heavy-set monuments which had seen me into the world, which would see me out of it, and whose permanence guaranteed me a future as calm as the past."[22] The meaning of the book is as much tied to its cumulative nature as its singularity. "Stacks" are a sign of the book's stability, the way in aggregate it acquires an architectural function. The book is also an infrastructure.

When I glance at a row of spines or a few briefly opened volumes, I am thinking about reading not only visually, but also speculatively. I am collecting "shoots" that might one day grow into something more robust. The outward turned spine is a site of potentiality, of what might be. Like medieval readers who were taught to put ideas in certain places in their minds, when

I browse I am locating ideas in physical space, to be returned to later. As in Sartre's account, stacks of books convey a sense of the durability of ideas.

Outsourcing browsing to our machines (that "browsers" are no longer people but programs) means that we are losing this sense of embodiment when it comes to browsing. As we meander our way through the web, our bodies are as inert as they were in the corner, but our minds are as energetic as before the book wheel. We are conflating two different kinds of reading that once belonged to two different spaces. In this, we are losing a sense of the differentiated time of reading, the long durations of the corner and the ambulatory, punctuated rhythms of the bookshelf. But we are also losing a sense of place. When we browse online, there are no corporal connections being made between what we've seen and where we've seen it. We have no physical and mental place to "put" our ideas gathered from our browsing, the results of our mental churning. Without books and their shelves, we lose a fundamental component of what it means to browse, to glance at books.

+ +

Today, reading is imagined to be everywhere. The idea of "pervasive computing" pervades how we think about the digital.[23] Where there is a computer, however small, there is something to be read. Miniaturization is no longer in the service of forgetting the book before you. It is a reminder that its computational twin is always there. Even in your toaster: Tatsuya Narita has invented a way to print out the day's weather from an RSS feed onto your morning toast (*Tenkipan*, 2009).

If digital texts are increasingly everywhere, they will also tell you where you are. "Locative media" has become one of the fastest growing segments of new reading tools, as GPS data is gradually integrated into our reading interfaces.[24] WikiMe arranges information not according to keyword, but by location. Citysense synthesizes data on the location of mobile device users and projects it onto a live map of urban activity. Fwix clusters news around physical locations so you can observe the information density of geographic spaces. Foursquare allows you to locate your friends to "catch up" with them. Graffitio creates virtual walls that correspond to real spaces where people can post "notes." When you approach these places your device will show you other people's postings. They can be practical and banal, but, like graffiti, at times deeply esoteric. They preserve, albeit in virtual form, a sense of mystery to urban reading.

In a world of locative media, it is increasingly hard to get lost, even for someone like me who is deeply navigationally challenged. (When I lived in New York my brother gave me a compass labeled Eastside/Westside and Uptown/Downtown for the four points of the compass. It was low-tech, but it worked.) In a world of mobile GPS devices, we are always somewhere. We read to catch up with others or be found by them. We no longer lose ourselves in our reading, like Augustine who for a brief moment heard the voice of God in his garden or the members of the zine *Punk* who wanted to piss on the establishment and start over.

Despite this intensification of place, digital reading can also feel like it is happening in many places at once. Perhaps this is what the vogue of locative media is all about. It is a corrective to the distributed nature of online reading. However much information may be place-bound, it is not necessarily the place where I am. Seeing where information dwells around the city or the world is a way of seeing oneself pulled in numerous directions. I am always "catching up," in the words of Foursquare. Unlike the compressions of the corner, reading online is centrifugal. This too has a printed past, as early eighteenth-century critics of the newspaper were fond of asking why readers in London cared about what was going on in faraway Poland or Sweden.[25] We read in and we read out.

Today, outward is definitely in. We increasingly speak of transmedia, transaesthetics, transdisciplinarity, the transfinite, and the transnational (well at least some of us do). The transitive property reins. Instead of all those things bumping into each other in the world of the "inter" (that bygone world of intermediality, interdisciplinarity, and, remember it? the Internet), we now just span. Ted Nelson's dream of "stretchtext" seems to have become the new standard.[26]

In new media artist Giselle Beiguelman's *Egoscópio* (2002), commercial billboards in São Paulo's high-tech district projected websites submitted by residents of the city. By giving these quasi-public spaces back to residents, her project was intended as a way of reconfiguring corporate ownership, "a hacking of the city structure," in Beiguelman's words.[27] But it was also a way of visualizing the increasingly distributed nature of reading. Even the billboard, that most static and monumental of reading spaces, was integrated into a broader geographic circuit. As a kind of massive urban playbill or broadside, the billboard in Beiguelman's work was shown to span social space.

Or consider the urban narrative project *Nonchalance* (2009), where readers participated in a story that took place across an entire city, in this case San Francisco. It was one of many such projects across the world that are known as alternative reality games, such as *Hundekopf* in Berlin or the series of works by Blast Theory in London or the Trans Reality Lab in Göteborg, Sweden. Consisting of everyday textual objects that routinely circulate in a city, such as flyers, tickets, sidewalk chalk drawings, or protest posters (fig. 6.7), as well as websites coordinated around real space, readers are led through stories tied to the historical identities of specific neighborhoods. The urban reader no longer seeks out the nook for the sake of getting lost, taking a rest, or taking a leak. He or she is now persistently on a quest for meaning.

Unlike the tourist for whom the book disappears before the monument and then reappears later as a space of memory, the new transitive nature of urban reading spans the space of the page and the real space behind it. There is a simultaneity about it, as it layers reading on top of real space in an interactive way. In so doing, it actively rewrites our sense of place. In William Shaw's *41 Places* (2007), for example, stories were installed in various locations around Brighton, England—a story about gay marriage

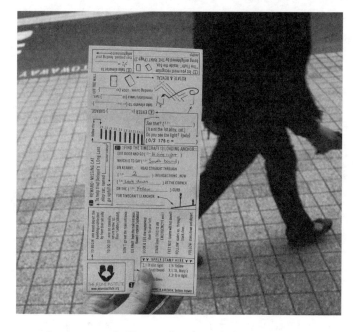

[FIGURE 6.7]   Image taken from the immersive game
Nonchalance (2009). Courtesy of the game's creator, Jeff Hull.

at the Town Hall, a story about a visitor looking at a painting of a
woman reading to her daughter at the Brighton Museum, a story
about a dropped cell phone at a local nightclub. It drew upon
the earlier work by Renate Stih and Frieder Schnock, *Places of
Remembrance* (1993), in which signs of anti-Semitic laws from
the Nazi period were recreated and placed in former Jewish quar-
ters of Berlin. In these urban reading experiments, which update
the graffiti art of the 1970s in more institutional terms, text and
place are ever more tightly woven together.

Such projects reconfigure reading not as a form of intimacy, as
an act of repose, but instead as one of focalization. As the creators
of *Nonchalance* argue, "It is in this space—this highly authentic,
reassuringly tangible 'real' world—that we're able to affect consciousness. Awareness is heightened; perspective altered."[28] But
this kind of situated reading is also understood as *transitional*,

in the sense of multisited. Reading "moves" us in a whole new way as we piece these relational parts together and move from one place to another. This is true now even when we sit down. In *Newscoons* (2008), which was shown at the National Art Museum in Beijing, chairs project aggregations of news from around the world, grouped by different keywords (body, alienation, recombinant, etc.).[29] Reading furniture no longer holds the text so that we may dream of somewhere else (or no place at all). The chair *is* the text, a text explicitly of and from somewhere else. The elsewhere is always a somewhere that is also right there. The transitive property reins.

+ +

Inside of every computer, at the very bottom of it all, lies a tree. The tree is one of the most elementary structures of all programming languages, whether it is the bifurcating nature of the if/then statement or the computational logic of the binary tree. The arboreal roots of the book have migrated into our computers, nicely turned outward in projects like Stefanie Posavec's "literary organisms," which turn books into treelike structures (fig. 6.8).[30]

Historians of ideas tell us that it was during the eighteenth century when the tree of knowledge began to give way to the knowledge "field."[31] Hierarchically ordered categories based on descending branches of knowledge were being replaced by adjacent, yet slightly porous fields. The sequentially ordered "leaf" was no longer at the center of learning; instead it was the topographical map. The foldout emerged as one of the premier textual instruments of the Enlightenment.[32] At the very moment that readers were heading out into the woods, in other words, the tree was already becoming a relic of thought. The computational tree has ironically only further accelerated the growth of knowledge fields.

Leaving the woods for the field has most often been thought of as a way of moving from darkness into light.[33] As Robert Harrison has written in his magnificent study on forests, "Forests recede

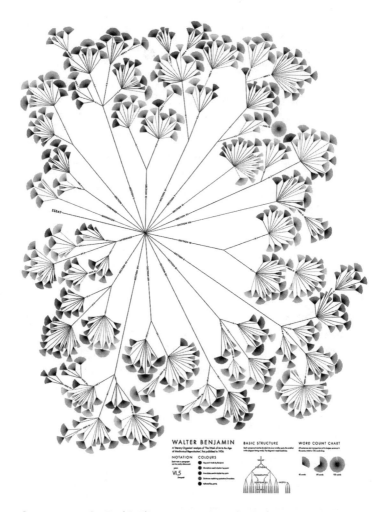

[FIGURE 6.8] In this "literary organism," by Stefanie Posavec, we see her signature visual analysis of Walter Benjamin's essay "The Work of Art in the Age of Mechanical Reproduction." Each branch corresponds to a section of the essay, and each leaf corresponds to a sentence. The size of the leaf displays the relative word length (the longest sentence in the essay is 126 words), while the colors of the leaves refer to five interpretive categories: key point, quotation, anecdote, explanation of quotation or anecdote, and italicized words. Courtesy of the artist.

from the civic horizon, appear through the pathos of distance, lengthen their shadows in the cultural imagination."[34] But leaving the forest for the field is also a move into a space of work. Unlike forests, fields must be tended. We may get lost in the woods, but fields make us tired, physically and visually. Fields extend beyond our lines of sight. They mark a horizon line. But fields also bring *ourselves* into view. In the field we are always exposed.

The rise of the field as a way of thinking about both knowledge and reading is one sign of how we have become fearful of reading's recesses. We are suspicious of the corner and the bower, of reading's folds. We are suspicious, I think, of the book's intimacy and its immeasurability.

As fields of knowledge continue to expand—as they continue to stretch beyond our capacity to know them in their entirety, as they continue to stretch *us*—there is a growing need to create more spaces for decompression. How can we imagine places of technology that generate repose and not just exposure? We need to remember the trees, not out of a false sense of naturalism, but for the type of place, and therefore the type of thinking, that they make possible. We need to remember the trellis (the canopy, the overhang, and the overstory) and not just the single tree (the trunk, the root, and the story). We need to remember the intermittent respite provided by the leaf.

There is reason here to be optimistic. Like museums, libraries are emerging as important actors within civic life. We have rediscovered just how important these pockets of reading are to the transitive properties of urban experience. Library attendance in North America is increasing, and library construction now stands as a showpiece of urban or regional renewal.[35] The bookstore, long thought dead, is being reimagined as a space of temporary respite, but also material encounter. In place of the timelessness of the independent store, like Shakespeare & Company, or the sheer inertia of the big-box store, like Barnes & Noble (at least it does seem to mark the end of the ampersand), in these newly reimagined spaces we are getting in touch with the stuff of reading—not just books but the numerous objects to which they are related. The bookstore is being reconceived as a space of transitory materialization.[36] Experiments in the creation of temporary libraries are emerging, too, like the Reanimation Library in New York that is comprised of a collection of books "deaccessioned" from public libraries or the Bedouin Library that is a traveling collection of works based on cultural stereotypes of the nomadic Arab. Even the bookmobile is making a comeback.[37] Reading, according to these examples, is becoming more situated, not in the sense of global "positioning," but rather in a more discontinuous, temporary, recessed kind of way—transitive, yet contained. Much like our eighteenth-century forebearers, we are trying to put place back into reading.

This past week we bought our daughter her first desk. This is where she tells us she will do her "bricolage"—all that experimental work with paper that includes glue, scissors, paint, stamps, ink, stickers, and anything else that can be minutely partitioned or chaotically aggregated. (When she comes down with her ink-stained hands I always imagine this is what it was like in the old days when a printer came home from work.) It is a material prelude to what she will one day do with the ideas she finds in books or online. But the desk is also about locating this kind of mental and physical labor in space. It is about containing the medley of our inner *bricoleur*. Virginia Woolf may have prioritized a room of one's own as the condition of a writer's or reader's life, but I personally think it starts with the desk. Who can forget one's first desk and the bizarre array of items it contained and that somehow belonged together?

When my daughter reads in the future, she will no doubt read more transitively than we have in the past. With her ubiquitous devices in tow, she will be in constant conversation with the ambient fields of digital agents surrounding her both near and far (cell towers, server farms, other human-bearing devices). She will know where she is when she reads, but so too will someone else. Reading will have a profound sense of place, even as place will be defined by a bifurcated sense of being both here and there. Her reading will be stretched.

But her reading will be stretched in another sense as well, in the sense of personal stress or pressure. The pressure of reading, that it can be anything but pleasurable at times, certainly predates the digital. Indeed, in many ways it is linked to that first technology, the *press*, that gave birth to the increased spread and functionalization of reading. But if Moore's law holds for transistors, then so too for reading. We have entered into an exponential relationship to the growth of reading material. Like many parents or educators, I worry that the growing expanse of reading pulls us apart, not just socially, but also personally. The incessant insistence on the functionality of reading—that there must be some "value" to it—only amplifies this problem. When there is so much more to read and when we are always reading for some purpose, we are only ever "catching up." We never have the chance to incorporate, digest, curl up, close off, recede.

In the next chapter, I will discuss some of the ways that individuals are developing tools to contend with this problem of the surplus of digital reading. It is here where we can see the emergence of new strategies for browsing and new ways of thinking about reading synoptically. But alongside reading's increasing sense of span, I also hope that there will continue to be way stations where my children can get lost for a bit, where they can lose a sense of place, where they can recoil. We need technologies, but also places, that contain such "data pores"[38]—not just synthetic spaces, but holes within the field, areas of immeasurability, pockets of discontinuity, one-way streets, dead ends, and hollows. For now, the book is still the ultimate data pore.

SEVEN

By the Numbers

In schools the math and writing master are usually one and
the same. But a master of writing books is seldom good at math.

JEAN PAUL [*the flailing years*]

Counting and recounting have been at the heart of reading since
its inception. The earliest forms of writing were notches on bones,
dating from around 30,000 BC. As in the biblical story of Adam's
rib, bones are where we record our debts. Clay tokens with symbols impressed upon them were used for the dual purposes of
accounting and recounting as far back as 8,000 BC in Turkey,
and in the Balkans the Vinča culture produced pottery with over
two hundred different symbols for similar ends around 5,000
BC. Even the earliest records of proto-alphabetic writing in the
third millennium were most often lists and ledgers used for counting purposes, a point no less true with the advent of literature.[1]
Whether it was Aesop's *Fables* or Mother Goose rhymes, *A Thousand and One Nights* or Boccaccio's *Decameron*, Poe's insistence
that composing "The Raven" was akin to solving a mathematical
problem, or even Spinoza's *Ethics* with its geometric proof of
the existence of God, the stories we tell ourselves are entwined
with the way we count. Literacy and numeracy are related to one
another at a deep anthropological level.

Counting has become a part of reading like never before. In a
world of computation, writing is fundamentally numerical, just

as reading has become a punctuated engagement with algorithmic process. When we read a digital text we are not reading a static object. We are reading one that has been generated through a set of procedural conditions that depend on our interaction with them. Digital texts are never just there. They are called forth through computation and interaction, whether by a human or a machine. This is what makes them dynamic, not static objects. It is this feature that marks the single strongest dividing line between the nature of books and that of their electronic counterparts.[2]

For many today, mathematical computation has become the negative pole of humanistic knowledge.[3] The "objectivity" produced by computation is not only deterministic, it no longer even needs us. Humanistic inquiry, by contrast, one premised above all on reading books, concerns the production of subjectivity, what it means to be a person in the world. The logical (and technological) determinacies of computation, so the argument goes, stand in stark opposition to the linguistic indeterminacies of reading books.

And yet the history of literature and its attachment to number, sequence, procedure, process, and form tells us a different story. Reading literature is indebted in profound ways to the world of the numerical, just as the history of mathematics is far from the deterministic horror story many make it out to be. Symbols like ∞, π, e, -2, $\sqrt{\ }$, $\approx$ or ideas like "plane," "circle," or "parallel line"— are these any more precise than when Mrs. Ramsay reads, "Nor praise the deep vermilion in the rose"? They are both signs of the necessity of form, of our need to model, approximate, represent. Whether as fiction or theorem, they are means of understanding a world that at bottom always seems to elude our grasp.

Can computation be thought of as part of reading? As part of the humanities? Must the humanities stand for human only? Are there ways to think in more elementary terms about the relationship between number, procedure, and words? Can we bridge this expanding gap between the computational and the literal and instead posit their intersection as a new core of intellectual life? Will this not be a prerequisite for the literacy of the future?

Part of understanding the future of reading will entail knowledge of the history of textual computation, the way we have done things to texts and the way texts have done things for us. We require a clearer sense of the notion of *process* as it relates to reading. Such thoughts move us from the nighttime of reading with which I began (dreaming in books), to reading's daytime (work and play). They return us to reading's numerological origins.

+ +

When Augustine opened the Bible at random and found the passage that changed his life, he was engaging in a time-honored practice. Readers routinely sought meaning from randomly accessed texts, one that in Augustine's day went by the name of *sortes Virgilianae* or Virgilian lots (so named because Virgil was its most popular source). The practice later came to be known more generally as "bibliomancy," divination by means of books. Like many readers, Augustine was combining chance and reading to arrive at a fundamental truth, one that was already there, but that could not be directly accessed. It required constraints, rules, and luck. It was a game. Augustine was playing his text.

With the advent of video games, game theory—ludology—has become a bedrock of new media studies.[4] In the often messianic rhetoric of reformers (beware the prophets), gaming will change our lives. "Games aren't leading us to the downfall of human civilization," writes Jane McGonigal in her gamer manifesto, *Reality Is Broken*. "They're leading us to its reinvention."[5]

This of course is nothing new. Games are some of the oldest forms of human practice, the idea of "Homo ludens" one of the recurring ways we have tried to understand our nature. "Man is only truly himself when he is at play," writes the playwright and sometime philosopher Friedrich Schiller in his epoch-making aesthetic theory written at the close of the eighteenth century. For Schiller, as for later philosophers like Johan Huizinga, "culture" was play's outcome, not something we created once we grew up.[6]

But there is also nothing new here in terms of reading. As the eminent Canadian critic Northrop Frye illustrated some time ago, the riddle is one of the oldest forms of literature.[7] It is thought to be a cognate of the verb to read, which derives from the Germanic root (*rādan*) for council, deliberation, but also conjecture. In taking time with language, in treating it as a game to be played, we learn to read. In European languages, riddles are some of the oldest forms of literature, from the tenth-century *Exeter Book*, which was an important source for the epic *Beowulf*, to the Icelandic *Hervarar Saga*, which utilized a popular form of question and answer as part of its narrative.[8]

The riddle depends upon a sense of intrigue, of a truth that is already there but when discovered feels new, sudden, miraculous. As André Jolles has suggested, the riddle is more about process than product.[9] Chance, not reason, reigns over such insights. I cannot deduce my way into the solution to the textual game, I can only stumble upon it. This truth, the one that appears by accident, is more profound, perhaps truer.

The history of how we have played with our books is a long one. In the thirteenth century, the Majorcan theologian Ramon Llull devised a system of overlapping rotatable discs that corresponded to a list of moral attributes and that drew heavily on an Arabic astrological device known as a *za'irja*. By rotating the discs, one could arrive at a number of fixed combinations of truths about the world drawn from sacred scripture. "The subject of this Art," writes Llull in a companion to his ultimate system, the *Ars Magna*, "is the answering of all questions, assuming that one can identify them by name."[10]

In the seventeenth century, the German poet Georg Harsdörffer produced a massive compendium of philosophical and mathematic games (like how to write on egg whites or calculate using letters).[11] One of his diversions was a so-called thought ring (fig. 7.1), which consisted of five separate layers of phonemes that allowed users to generate all possible combinations of the German language—and of course many more (97,209,600 in all). Language and the ideas that emerged from it were understood in

[FIGURE 7.1] The "thought ring" from Georg Philipp
Harsdörffer, *Deliciae Physico-Mathematicae* (1651), 517.
Courtesy of the Klassik Stiftung Weimar, HAAB/G4:14.

a combinatory sense according to Harsdörffer's acutely baroque
sensibility. Breaking down language into parts and then playing
with these units was the condition of bringing new words, and
presumably new ideas, into the world. Harsdörffer's thought ring
was an instrument, to be played in much the same way as the popular harpsichord was in his day. Unlike Llull's discs that always
brought you back to the same scriptural truths, Harsdörffer's
had the potential to deliver you into a world of novelty, the un-
thought and the unsaid, and of course the unsayable—nonsense
was always a possible outcome of the "ring." Nonsense was the
flipside of novelty.

However much Harsdörffer's thought ring was an idle pastime for the salons and drawing rooms of the well-to-do, it also drew upon the more popular genre of "counting-out" rhymes that one finds across the world's cultures and that depend on the use of meaningless words: eeny meeny miny mo, hakara bakara, essike tessike, pico pico masa rico, and so on. At the very basis of computation, of "counting out," is linguistic nonsense. But so too is death. Not only are these rhymes related to the process of drawing lots, they are often interchangeable with incantations recited over the dying.[12] "Ena, mena, bora, mi," begins one English rhyme that ends with the words, "Stick, stock, stone dead." Counting *out*, deciding who is "it," is the symbolic rehearsal of our own mortality.

At the opening of the twentieth century, two of the founders of the Dada movement, Francis Picabia and Tristan Tzara, sat down in front of each other one evening to write spontaneous, and nonsensical, prose poems on opposite sides of a page.[13] They were arguing (once again) for chance and play as the core principles of creative writing. As Tzara asked in his manifesto, "How can one expect to put order into the chaos that constitutes the infinite and shapeless variation of man?"[14] In Tzara's hands the page was the imaginative equivalent of the spinning wheel.

Less than twenty years later, the mathematician and key founder of the modern computer Alan Turing would reflect on how a text could become a machine. His insight was to translate writing from the two-dimensional space of the page to the one-dimensional line of tape. "Computing is normally done by writing certain symbols on paper," writes Turing in one of the most important papers in the history of computing. "I think it will be agreed that the two-dimensional character of paper is no essential of computation. I assume then that the computation is carried out on one-dimensional paper, i.e. on a tape."[15] The combinatory arts of the wheel were united in Turing with the serial procedures of the tape, redeploying the age-old textual metaphor of the "spool" (incidentally one of Samuel Beckett's most beloved words from

Krapp's Last Tape). At the dawn of computing the scroll returns, an ironic bookend to the end of the book.

The term we use for such computational procedures is "algorithm," named after the ninth-century Arabic mathematician Mohammed ibn-Musa al-Khwarizmi. As David Berlinski tells us, "An algorithm is an effective procedure, a way of getting something done in a finite number of discrete steps."[16] On the one hand, algorithms can be very precise, like the Google search engine that more often than not returns exactly what you are looking for. But algorithms can also be the means of producing surprise, of something unexpected. Harsdörffer's thought ring is one such example. Critics have recently begun to call for a more creative relationship to the use of algorithms, to expand our sense of the "query" or "search" beyond the highly restricted outcomes of Google or its competitors.[17] Other than the "feeling lucky" option, there is remarkably little play when we search online.

A number of creative writers have begun experimenting with computational algorithms, what Noah Wardrip-Fruin calls "textual instruments" or Kenneth Goldsmith "uncreative writing," in order to rediscover a sense of linguistic surprise. "The world is full of texts, more or less interesting," writes Goldsmith. "I do not wish to add any more."[18] Instead of writing books or texts, writers now write the rules that make books or texts. They write writing machines. As a set of rules, the algorithm is imagined to be the tool that will paradoxically rescue us from the overly rule-based nature of computational writing, to reintroduce chance and play into our highly structured textual universe. In this, I can't help but think of Goethe's play *Tasso*, whose poetic hero clings at the close of the play to the worldly prince on whom he depends for his well-being. In his last moments, he remarks, "And so at the very last the helmsman clings fast to the rock on which he foundered."[19] The algorithm is the rock that rescues us from the shipwreck of computation.

There are a variety of new projects on offer whose aim is to scramble our overly formatted textual flow. In Wardrip-Fruin's

News Reader (2004), for example, an algorithm synthesizes se-mantically related pieces of news to create entirely new articles. By clicking on headlines drawn from RSS feeds, his instrument takes stories from other sources and gradually builds new pieces, so that reading is also a form of writing. The articles that emerge are, in a very ancient sense, woven together. The more we play, the more they entwine, the further we are from "the news" and the closer we are to "the new" (and also nonsense, which is never far away from play).

In a more literary vein, the new media artist D. Fox Harrell has created GRIOT, a computational narrative program named after West African storytellers that is designed to produce hai-buns, or prose haikus. These short linguistic snapshots are gener-ated from users' inputs that are then run through a combinatory algorithm:

> save us from desire, tender
> fixed, forgotten

> save us from fear, wanting
> addict & moonlight

They can be quite beautiful, arranging the linguistic jumble of our lives into meaningful configurations, much like latter-day medieval books of hours or baroque sonnets. As Mrs. Ramsay said of the sonnet, so too of the algorithmic haibun: "How satis-fying! How restful! All the odds and ends of the day stuck to this magnet."[20] This is how the new magnet, the hard drive, speaks, with the day's semantic filings arranged into meaningful patterns. It is an ideal textual companion of the future, Virgilian lots for the computational age.

In Darren Wershler and Bill Kennedy's *Apostrophe Engine* (2001), clicking on a line of Kennedy's poem "Apostrophe" sub-mits it to a web-based search engine that collects all phrases that begin with the words, "you are," and then assembles them in sequential order. "Apostrophe" is the rhetorical term for direct address (Dear reader, hey you, O Death!), and the results produce lines like "You are a dog on a leash like a pig in a pen," "You are not doing it right, you damn well know you are doing it wrong," or "You are really depressed and you just want to shout 'SHUT UP! SHUT UP! SHUT UP!'"[21] Every line is itself clickable so that the poem is as potentially large as the web itself. It represents the sum of what we say we are online.

Much of this work—and there is much more of it—goes back to the experiments of John Cayley, one of the forerunners of constructing textual instruments. For Cayley, whose projects depend on what he calls "transliteral morphing," the algorithm is used less for the purposes of surprise and more to reveal deeper patterns between words and letters. The semantic nonsense that his projects like *Riverisland* (2007) and *Overboard* (2004) produce are there to help us see the more elementary relationships between the shapes and sounds of letters.[22] Surface noise, intellectual depth, and "going overboard"—these are the core elements of computational reading, what it takes to see form in our massively overburdened textual lives.

Time and again projects like these are pejoratively referred to as "mere games." Unlike cinema, photography, or books—each with its own aesthetic highs to its more entertainment-laden lows—digital games have not made their way into the expression industry in any canonical sense, this despite the fact that they can constitute huge textual units (one recent game, Dragon Age, consists of over 1.2 million words). However brilliant early text-based adventure games were, we still have no Proust of Zork. I do not mean this ironically. Imagine if you could play *In Search of Lost Time*. It would be amazing.

When it comes to reading today, we seem to be distrustful of play and the constraints it requires. We tend to privilege virtuosity over failure. For the Dadaist Francis Picabia, whose favorite journal was subtitled *Le Raté*, or *The Failure*, the pending arrival of our success-obsessed age was already palpable. He could sense how fearful we were becoming of non-sense, the nonreal, the absence of purpose (or in the words of a fellow traveler:

beware of the "literary quacks with a mania for improvement"). In response, a variety of new media artists are taking as their starting point the dysfunctionality of computation, the way electronic technologies, unlike books, are prone to break down.[23] It is no surprise that the "outtake," the genre of deleted scenes, has emerged as an essential new form today. It is success culture's obscene matter.

And yet playing with texts has always been at the heart of reading. It is a crucial way that we interact with strings of words, the way we make sense of the world's polyphony. Playing with texts is how we encounter the limits of sense, meaning's blurry edges. It has been there from the start of reading, and it is at the core of some of the greatest works of the modern age: *Faust*, *Ulysses*, *The Making of Americans*, *Gravity's Rainbow*, but also Dada, Oulipo, Fluxus, and the Ramones. The algorithm is the riddle's heir.

When we read a book we are reading someone else's modeling of an artificial world, whether real or imagined. We are reading virtuosity, the skill with which someone is able to create ex nihilo. When we read a game, we are reading someone else's interpretation of how *we* model the world. We are reading an interpretation of human creativity. In playing with textual games, we learn about our own thought processes, about the nature of expression, about the formal structures of language-based reason. Through the algorithm we learn about learning, the success of failure.

+ +

That was play, this is work.

I want to conclude this chapter and my book, but hopefully not *the* book, with a discussion of a new set of computational reading practices. They date back in many ways to the 1970s, a computational high-water mark for many disciplines. But they are only now gradually beginning to alter the landscape of professional reading, what used to be known as philology and now goes by the name of digital humanities.[24] It is not without its detractors.

But then again, when has this not been the case when there have been changes to how we read?

First, some examples. FeatureLens, which was developed by the Human-Computer Interaction Lab at the University of Maryland, is a program that allows you to view meaningful semantic patterns within large structures of texts (fig. 7.2). For Tanya Clement, who undertook an analysis of Gertrude Stein's famously difficult and repetitive novel *The Making of Americans* (1925), the interface revealed a range of structural patterns so far unnoticed by readers.[25] Using FeatureLens, Clement was able to see the symmetrical repetition of certain phrases, the way "any such a thing" appears exactly ten times in each of the chapters where it appears. She also noticed that the repetition of the single longest

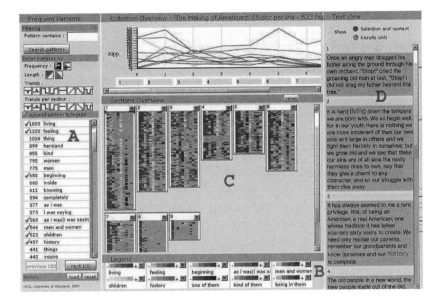

[FIGURE 7.2]   An image of the interface FeatureLens, taken
from Tanya Clement, "'A thing not beginning and not ending':
Using Digital Tools to Distant Read Gertrude Stein's *The Making
of Americans,*" *Literary and Linguistic Computing* 23, no. 3
(2008): 364. By permission of Oxford University Press.

string of words (495 in all) occurs only once at the exact mid-point of the novel, suggesting that the novel has a cyclical rather than random structure. And finally, her research showed that the repetitions of the last chapter are not unique to that chapter, as is the case with the other chapters, but appear scattered throughout the novel. Far from articulating a principle of randomness, this last detail suggests how the final chapter assumes the structure of a refrain (called a "rhapsody" by Stein). Rather than marking an end point, it is the moment when the novel circles back on itself. There is a virtuosity to Stein's play that takes place at a remarkable level of scale and that only becomes visible when subjected to such quantitative inquiry.

In John Mohr and Vincent Duquenne's work on the history of poverty, by using quantitative techniques they were able to show how changes in the discourse of poverty—the words used to describe it—corresponded to historical changes in the institutional practices used to address it.[26] Examining the clusters of words related to poverty (needy, distressed, worthy, indigent, destitute) and the actions to which they corresponded at two major turning points in the history of social welfare (between the end of the poorhouse era in the 1880s and the beginnings of the welfare state in the 1910s), their work is aimed at helping us understand the rationale behind changing types of institutional relief programs. Their research reveals a historical correlation between words and deeds, not only how a given moment understands what it is doing, but how words also help produce those actions.

Finally, in my own project that relies on computational textual analysis, I am interested in creating literary "topologies," or historical maps, of literary networks. The first suite of maps will be called *The Werther Effect*, based on Goethe's novel *The Sorrows of Young Werther* (1774), one of the most popular literary works of the eighteenth century (often referred to as the first European "best seller").[27] While we have a number of bibliographies that list the many adaptations of *Werther* that followed in its wake (over two hundred by some estimates), we still have very little sense of the extent to which *Werther* fanned out into the world of eighteenth-century letters more broadly. If *Werther* was, as one critic has put it, a "syndrome" of the emerging middle-class commercial culture to which it belonged, I want to know more about the reach of the text's pathos.[28] The question is not simply to what extent the novel infected the language of its age, but more challengingly, *in what ways* did it do so—what was the nature of *Werther*'s influence, in terms of its language and style, that suffused the closing decades of the period known as the Enlightenment?

To try to answer these questions, my collaborator, Mark Algee-Hewitt, and I are using statistical models to compare lexical "thumbprints" of *Werther* with other eighteenth-century works and then projecting those relationships as a network map (fig. 7.3). In measuring the prevalence of the most common words in *Werther*—its lexical identity—*within* other works from the period (eventually about five thousand), we can see where a work like *Werther* "goes" and the types of clusters or new arrangements of texts that it helps produce. We can observe a kind of structuring effect that *Werther*'s language has on the period. But we can also gain a better sense of how it travels, the specific aspects of *Werther* that contribute to these new textual communities. By focusing on smaller units such as the page, the paragraph, the sentence, or even the phoneme or morpheme (such as prefixes and suffixes), we can zoom in to see which aspects of *Werther* are doing the work of bringing certain groups of texts together. But we can also turn the question around and ask where a work like *Werther* comes from. If the novel supposedly undergoes a "rise" in the eighteenth century, where did it originate? Is it more or less like other novels, newspapers, biographies, or philosophy? How "new" was it? Whatever the answers may be, these are questions we simply cannot reliably answer by hand (though we have tried).

The kind of work I've been describing here, and again there is much more of it, largely falls under the heading of "distant reading."[29] In place of the "close reading" that analyzed a single work in great detail, the former bedrock of literary criticism, we

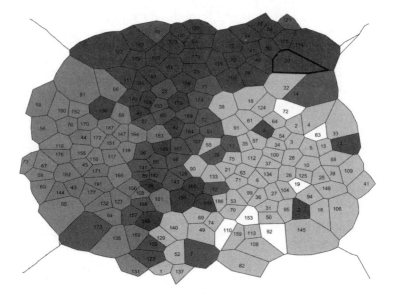

[FIGURE 7.3] Andrew Piper and Mark Algee-Hewitt, The *Werther Effect* (2011). Presented is a topological map of Goethe's collected works, arranged in their relationship to his youthful novel *The Sorrows of Young Werther*. The map is color-coded according to genre, with novels and autobiography located mostly at the top, dramatic works to the lower right, critical essays making a streak down the middle, and his science writings comprising the far left. The further apart any two tiles are, the less alike they are, and the smaller the tile, the more it resembles those works directly surrounding it. *Werther* is the highlighted tile in the upper right corner. The map is reproduced courtesy of Mark Algee-Hewitt.

are now reading a great many works together (or not reading them, as both detractors and promoters alike are fond of saying). But on another level, we could say that distant reading is in practice just another form of close reading, perhaps the closest kind. It is intensely word based, far closer to older reading practices like medieval gloss, which attempted to explicate a text word for word. As many have pointed out, it is indebted to textual instruments like the concordance, which was first used in the thirteenth century and which arranges words from a larger corpus (initially the Bible) into an alphabetical list.[30]

These projects are premised on the idea that reading "just the words" is not a primitive model of how we read, but a fundamental one. The attention to individual words is driven by the idea that our experience when we read is at its most meaningful prior to any theoretical abstractions that we produce through these words (as they coalesce into things like plot, character, or the text's "message"). Words are what our minds embrace, follow, puzzle over. They are the clay, the raw material, the *pleasure* of reading. But such distant readings are also a means of understanding the meaning of linguistic *recurrence*, how words repeat themselves at a distance and how these gradual accumulations of repetition are essential for the way texts accrue meaning. Such distant readings are in many ways closer in spirit to the poetic device of the refrain, one of the oldest tools for lending words meaning. When Edgar Allen Poe was deciding upon the feature that would make "The Raven," which would subsequently be considered one of the most important poems in the English language, universally accessible he chose the single word refrain, "Nevermore."[31] Understanding the differences within language's repetitions is one of reading's backbones.

For all of this newfound idolatry of the word, however, these types of projects also argue for a kind of reading that is deeply visual. We *look* at a topology or a graph in order to gain a sense of the whole. However visual our relationship to reading books may be, unlike a topology a book can never be read all at once. This is the point of the haunting images by the visual artist Idris Khan that consist of the pages of books superimposed onto one another and that are illegible. A book insists on either sequence or slice. A book takes time. The computational interface, by contrast, tries to give access to a totality, to present sequence *as* slice. It recalls reading's other etymological origin, not as a riddle, but as a form of agricultural harvesting or gathering together. As the father of hermeneutics, Friedrich Schleiermacher, argued at the turn of the nineteenth century, "Without the whole no true understanding is possible."[32]

As a consequence, computational interfaces like the topology immerse us into a world of likeness rather than one of distinction. They ask us to think about words and works in relation to one another. Where books are tools of distinction, "difference engines" as I called them in the last chapter, topologies teach us to understand the meaning of connectivity, of the "next to." They place us in a more critical relationship to the "network" as one of the dominant figures of contemporary thought. As John Cayley intuited, language always goes overboard; its meaning runs past the artificial boundaries we establish to contain it. Distant reading is the attempt to hang on to the ballast of words against which we as readers inevitably, frustratingly, and at times joyfully founder.

+ +

At the opening of the sixteenth century, the great Renaissance man of letters Erasmus of Rotterdam published a new version of the New Testament. In two separate columns, he arranged the earliest Greek sources alongside Jerome's Latin translation, known as the Vulgate Bible and the official edition of the Catholic Church. Erasmus's edition, as one might imagine, was controversial. But in many ways he was following the lead of his fourth-century predecessor Jerome, who had returned to the Hebrew sources for his translation of the Old Testament. And Jerome, for his part, was following the lead of the third-century Egyptian scholar Origen, whose Hexapla, a six-column comparison of the Hebrew and Greek sources of the Bible, had served as an important basis for Jerome's translation.[33]

Whether it was Erasmus, Jerome, or Origen, each of these scholars was taking apart an earlier text and putting it back together in new ways for the purpose of reading it in new ways.

In the nineteenth century, the philologist Karl Lachmann would begin to do the same for the origins of Germanic literature. Undoing and redoing a rich vernacular heritage, he gave birth to what has come to be known as "the critical edition," the foundational object for all professional reading.[34]

We are at a similar moment in terms of creating new textual instruments today. Current anxieties about the meaning of computational interfaces are no different than the controversies that surrounded the biblical translations of Renaissance humanists. Erasmus had provocatively entitled his edition *Novum Instrumentum*, not *Novum Testamentum*, a new instrument, not a new testament. For Erasmus, the book was indeed an instrument, not just a "mere tool." Where some readers were shocked to encounter his edition rather than Jerome's, so too are some readers today just as shocked to see their beloved Jane Austen heaped onto a giant pile of books and run through the mill of data mining. We continue to struggle with the idea of writing as an instrument and not as a testament.

Such computational reading is in large part a response to the growing quantity of things to read. There has, of course, always been too much to read. But with the digital preservation of Twitter (177 million tweets per day), Google Books (15 million books), or the Internet more generally (who knows), we have entered a new order of magnitude of "too much." To read all of this, to preserve any sense of synopsis that Schleiermacher had suggested was the very condition of understanding, we will need new instruments and new methods of reading. The book isn't enough.

It is, in my view, an exciting time. Whether as professionals or amateurs, there is an opportunity here for readers to get their hands dirty, to reimagine the shape of our reading instruments, like Peter Organisciak's recent TAToo (for Text Analysis Tool), which can be imbedded alongside a text in your browser so that you have a running word cloud, concordance, and list of collocates for whatever you happen to be reading at the moment. It is the latest example of what Stéfan Sinclair calls "ubiquitous analysis."[35] If we are going to have enhanced books that distract us with animation and soundtracks, we might as well have ones that help us think more analytically about what we're reading, too.

As I've tried to argue throughout this book, the point of such work is not to "overcome" older ways of reading. Reading can never be progressive. But it can show us how computational reading is different from book reading, how we can do different things with these different instruments, one no better than the other. The categories that I have laid out above—the lexical, visual, synoptic, and relational emphases of the computational interface—are a starting point for thinking through how computation will impact how we read. Perhaps the term we need then is not distant reading, but multiple reading—the way computation stacks different types of reading on top of one another. This too has its origins in book culture, not only in its indebtedness to the shape of the pile or stack, but in the way one of the book's historical strengths as a technology has been its ability to be used in so many diverse ways. We don't need more reading, just more *kinds* of reading. As in an ecosystem, diversity is a sign of a system's health.

In my preface to this book I mentioned that when I was a child I went to computer camp. While there I was taught to read the language of a machine and understand its logic. I have since forgotten much of what I learned, but I am now in the process of relearning it, bit by bit (so to speak). Many years later, while in graduate school, I went to book camp, actually the Rare Book School at the University of Virginia, one of the premier centers for the study of the book. It was there that I learned to read the codes of how books work. In many ways it was surprising, but also refreshing, to know more about the instrument that I spent so much of my time unconsciously using. It was also the beginning of my understanding of the extent to which our digital future is indelibly linked to our bibliographic past.

When I finish writing today, I will pick up our children from school. Today is my turn for the whirlwind of packing, zipping, searching, undressing, and cooking that marks the end of "work." My son is now completing first grade, and over the time it has taken me to write this book he has learned how to read. Like millions of other children his age, his mental universe has been permanently reshaped. He will never look on the world in quite the same way. And yet this is still not true for everyone. Whether because of disability or disadvantage, not all children (or adults) have equal access to reading. According to the United Nations, close to one-fifth of the world's population cannot read. In the United States, 13 percent of school-age children have some kind of learning disability that negatively impacts their reading. And a growing portion of the adult population is falling behind in terms of functional literacy.[36] Reading is not, and has never been, universal. Part of the aim of books like this one is to remind us just how much work reading requires to sustain itself.

When my son comes home today, he will play with the computer. Then he will go and do his homework, where he will use books for his reading, writing, and math exercises. My daughter, who is still in preschool, will simulate this process in reverse, playing with her notebooks, while the computer is still very much work for her. My hope is that these two categories, work and play, will remain as interwoven throughout their lives as the instruments that they use to engage in them, the book and the computer. I hope they are afforded the advantages of both, and that they pass on those advantages to others. My real hope, though, is that when it comes time to learn how these two very different instruments work (and play), I can send them to just one camp.

Letting Go of the Book

What? Still amusing yourself with a book?
This isn't Sunday, you know.
MARCEL PROUST [*in search of lost time*]

Books are never finished.
PAUL AUSTER [*red notebook*]

What would the world be like without books? It turns out this is a very old question. We have already seen many examples over the course of this book. In the third century, the Egyptian scholar Origen created a six-columned reading device, a superbook, for comparing the Hebrew and Greek sources of the Bible. In the thirteenth century, the Majorcan scholar Ramon Llull imagined the book first in the shape of a tree and then as a series of spinning discs. In the nineteenth century, the German satirist Jean Paul conceived of the book as one long, unfurling piece of paper consisting of a single line of poetic prose (or prosaic poetry). He said it would make no small impression were it attached to the back of a child, like angel's wings, or a juvenile sail made from diaper cloth.[1]

At the end of the nineteenth century, the French symbolist poet Stéphane Mallarmé suggested that "all earthly existence must ultimately be contained in a book."[2] Neither many columned nor extremely long, the book was to be as large as the entire universe.

In the twentieth century, the Russian modernist filmmaker Sergei Eisenstein imagined a spherical book, the only proper form for his critical writings on cinema. There has even been an idea for a "book in a can," an inspired student project of a scroll stuffed into a metal container now preserved in the rare books collection at McGill University. Ever since its inception, it seems, we have been dreaming beyond the book.

In 2005, as part of an installation that would later show at the Guggenheim Museum, the acclaimed Palestinian artist Emily Jacir shot one thousand books using a .22 caliber pistol. *Material for a Film*, as it was called, was designed to commemorate the assassination of the Palestinian intellectual Wael Zuaiter, who was killed by Israeli intelligence agents in reprisal for the slaying of eleven Israeli athletes at the Munich Olympics in 1972. At the time of his death, Zuaiter was carrying a copy of *A Thousand and One Nights*, which he was translating into Italian. Shot thirteen times, one of the bullets hit his copy of the book. The book now resides in the Wael Zuaiter Center in Massa Carrara, Tuscany.

In Jacir's installation the book proved to be an affecting symbol for the defenseless scholar caught up in a world of violent exchange. It was a poignant reminder of Heinrich Heine's famous remark that where books are burned, people will soon follow. But Jacir's work was also part of a larger wave of contemporary projects that were performing aggressive, even violent, acts toward books.[3] Cutting, drowning, soaking, unfurling, piercing, and shooting books have been some of the many ways that artists like Jacqueline Rush Lee, Jonathan Latham, Robert The, Cara Barer, and Sam Markham have over the past decade or more been enacting a collective sense of the book's immanent demise (fig. 8.1). If we have forever been imagining our way past books, we have more recently begun to think about what it would be like to live in a world without them. We have begun the work of bibliographic mourning.

At an even deeper level, though, Jacir's work and the work of other book demolishers isn't just about a particular moment in

[FIGURE 8.1]   Sam Markham, from the series *In a Cold Winter* (2002). Courtesy of the artist.

time when the book's viability as a medium seems to be increasingly in doubt. It also captures something fundamental to the act of reading itself, something more timeless about the kindred spirits of mourning and melancholy that go with reading. Just as the imagination of how to transcend books has been integral to the history of books, so too is a sense of melancholy, a persistent sense of loss. Melancholy isn't a sign of the book's end; it is its inspiration. Melancholy is reading's muse.

"All my reading is nothing," remarked the German Enlightenment philosopher Johann Georg Hamann, nicknamed the Magus of the North. "Nothing but to make me duller and increase my boredom and make me despondent." Or as he wrote in another letter to a friend, "Incessant reading is as much a punishment for me as carrying water through a sieve was for the Danaïdes."[4] In his monumental work *The Anatomy of Melancholy*, the seventeenth-century scholar Robert Burton counted reading as one of the primary causes of melancholy. According to one classical rhyme on the matter collected by Burton, the common effects of reading included

> Grief, labor, care, pale sickness, miseries,
> Fear, filthy poverty, hunger that cries,
> Terrible monsters to be seen with the eyes.[5]

When the Visigoths invaded Greece and were intent on burning their books, one of the conquering generals is rumored to have cried out, "Leave them that plague. In time it will consume all their vigor and martial spirits."[6]

If a sense of melancholy often surrounds reflections on the future of reading—including my own, I confess it has been impossible to resist—it is because melancholy belongs so fundamentally to the experience of reading. There is ultimately a sadness to reading, not only because it is so nonvital, sluggish, or even deadening. Reading also bears with it a sense of some impossibility, a finitude that no amount of technological innovation will ever fix. What Augustine said of the angels—"they are always reading and what they read never comes to an end"—is never true for us. Letting go belongs as much to the past as it does the future of the book. In the end, we must always let go of the book.

+ +

Over the course of this book I have tried to give many reasons for why reading books has been, and in my opinion continues to be, important. One of the reasons I have most often encountered is the power of redundancy. Books have been important to us because of the way our interactions with them span several domains of sensory and physical experience. Whether it is through the acts of touch, sight, sound, sharing, or acquiring a sense of place, these embodied, and at times interpersonal, ways of interacting with books coalesce to magnify the learning that takes place through them. The same information processed in different ways and woven together is one of the profound secrets of bookish thought.

In his influential account of the birth of writing, Walter Ong argued that redundancy was a core feature of oral cultures, but one that diminished with the onset of writing (you don't need to repeat that which you've written down).[7] According to Ong, and many writers who have come in his wake, writing allows for more originality and individuality. And yet even if it is true that written documents contain lower degrees of redundancy than oral narratives (a big if), I think it is safe to say that literate cultures are skilled producers of extraordinary amounts of redundancy. Whether through the practice of manual or mechanical copying or the live performance of written texts, redundancy is reinscribed in literate societies at the level of circulation. One only needs to think about the voluminous amount of copies in circulation today (or during the earlier spread of print) to get some idea of how persistent redundancy is to modern forms of communication. Redundancy is not something that only belongs to "primitive" cultures; it is a basic condition of communicative reliability, of producing mutual understanding. Indeed, as the field of bioinformatics has more recently taught us, it is an elementary condition of life itself.[8]

The significance of redundancy for human communication is to my mind one of the most persuasive reasons why the printed book should still matter to us today. But it is also a compelling argument for the importance of new forms of electronic reading. Expanding the number of channels through which our ideas circulate makes those ideas potentially richer. That was the lesson of medieval manuscript illustrations that we saw in chapter 1 that highlighted the intersection of books, scrolls, and human speech to achieve a greater sense of understanding. And it was also the lesson of those lab rats I mentioned in chapter 4, who weren't able to integrate different kinds of information such as "blue" and "left" into a single, more complex idea. More aspects of communication are not just quantitatively different. They are also *qualitatively* different. Whether it is blue/left or book/computer, these multiple channels synthesize into something greater than the sum of their parts. The aggregation, and not the singularization, of communication is the condition of more complex thought. It is the condition of our humanity. Remember the rats.

At the turn of the nineteenth century, the German naturalist Alexander von Humboldt imagined putting "the entire material world in a single book."[9] Humboldt's obsessions with the *Über-buch* (his last was tellingly titled *Kosmos*) stood in stark contrast to his life's work devoted to promoting an ecological understanding of the earth's natural diversity. Where he saw complex arrangements of plant life, he saw just one form of communication, the printed book.

Humboldt was writing for an age that in many ways gave birth to our current obsession with books. While the book had been around for over a millennium and half by Humboldt's day, it was only at the turn of the nineteenth century when we witness a marked and mostly continual quantitative increase in the number of books, an increase that corresponded to a profound emotional investment in books as objects. Whether understood as plagues, earthquakes, or even things one could marry, the extent of the book's impact on us was imagined to be vast, deep, and lasting.

But that very ubiquity—the way the book emerged as one of the single most important cultural objects after 1800—was a function of its integration with *other* ways of expressing ourselves (the theater, visual arts, polite conversation, or writing by hand).[10] The book was imagined to be a single, all-encompassing medium. And yet this belied the truth of its own heterogeneity and the diverse ways it was woven within a broader field of communication. The book didn't kill, as Victor Hugo once famously claimed, it coordinated.[11] The book was, and has always been, part of an ecosystem, the very idea of which we owe to people like Alexander von Humboldt.

The story of the book's dominance in the nineteenth century should stand as an important reminder to us today. As we are overrun by computation, much in the same way as we were once overrun by books, we need to remember that what makes us unique as a species is our ability not just to communicate in complex ways through words. It is our ability to layer—or more artisanally understood, to weave—different modes of communication with one another to give those same words a deeper, more profound meaning. While everyone is searching for the magical potion of convergence—the single gadget that can perform all of our computational tasks, like the universal remote control—I think there should be those of us who are continually on the lookout for new communicative species, like the herb hunters in the Amazon today and like Humboldt before them. We may need to put down the book from time to time, but we should make sure not to let the computer become the new book. The universal medium, like the universal library, is a dream that does more harm than good.

NOTES

PROLOGUE

1. Some highlights: Alberto Manguel, *A History of Reading* (New York: Viking, 1996); Guglielmo Cavallo and Roger Chartier, eds., *A History of Reading in the West* (Amherst: University of Massachusetts Press, 1999); and Leah Price, "Reading: The State of the Discipline," *Book History* 7 (2004): 303–20. On the neuroscience of reading, see Stanislas Dehaene, *The Reading Brain: The Science and Evolution of a Human Invention* (New York: Viking, 2009), and Maryanne Wolf, *Proust and the Squid: The Story and Science of the Reading Brain* (New York: Harper, 2008).

2. As Michael Keller, director of Stanford University's Libraries, recently remarked about students, "They write their papers online. They read articles online. Many, many, many of them read chapters of books online. I can see in this population of students behaviors that clearly indicate where this is all going." Laura Sydell, "Stanford Ushers in the Age of Bookless Libraries," National Public Radio, July 8, 2010, http://www.npr.org/templates/story/story.php?storyId=128361395.

3. See Nicholas Carr, *The Shallows: What the Internet Is Doing to Our Brains* (New York: Viking, 2010), and Naomi Baron, *Always On: Language in an Online and Mobile World* (Oxford: Oxford University Press, 2010).

4. The fear that there would not be enough readers (and paper) for all the new authors was voiced by Johann Georg Meusel in his eighteenth-century encyclopedia on all living German writers, *Das Gelehrte Teutschland*, vol. 12 (Lemgo: Meyer, 1806), lxiv. As Christoph Martin Wieland, another contemporary, remarked, "If everyone writes, who will read?" Here is the sentiment in updated form: "Never have so many people written so much to be read by so few." Katie Hafner, "For Some, the Blogging Never Stops," *New York Times*, May 27, 2004, sec. G1. The death of publishing via self-publishing was declared around the most famous case in the eighteenth century, when Friedrich Klopstock, then the German language's best-known poet, started his own subscription service (it failed). And the fear that people wouldn't read books anymore (in this case because of newspapers) was voiced by August Prinz in *Der Buchhandel vom Jahre 1815 bis zum Jahre 1843* (Altona: Verlags-Bureau, 1855), 26. As scholars like Peter Stallybrass and Leah Price have reminded us, the book has at least since the invention of printing been a minor player in quantitative terms within a larger world of print. As Price writes, "There's nothing new, then, about the book's precarious perch within a larger media ecology." See Leah Price, "Reading as if for Life," *Michigan Quarterly Review* 48, no. 4 (2009): 483–98, and Peter Stallybrass, "'Little Jobs': Broadsides and the Printing Revolution," in *Agents of Change: Print Culture Studies after Elizabeth L. Eisenstein*, ed. Sabrina A. Baron, Eric N. Lindquist, and Eleanor F. Shevlin (Amherst: University of Massachusetts Press, 2007).

5. A great deal of recent work has tried to develop ways of thinking about media "ecologies" rather than focus on any one particular medium in isolation. See, for example, the work of Matthew Fuller, *Media Ecologies: Materialist Energies in Art and Technoculture* (Cambridge, MA: MIT Press, 2005); N. Katherine Hayles, "Intermediation: The Pursuit of a Vision," *New Literary History* 38, no. 1 (2007): 99–125; Dick Higgins, *Horizons: The Poetics and Theory of Intermedia* (Carbondale: Southern Illinois University Press, 1984); and the ongoing work of our research group in Montreal, "Interacting with Print: Cultural Practices of Intermediality, 1700–1900," http://interactingwithprint.org/.

6. Alexis Weedon, ed., *A History of the Book in the West*, 5 vols. (Burlington, VT: Ashgate, 2010); Michael F. Suarez, SJ, and H. R. Woudhuysen, eds., *The Oxford Companion to the Book*, 2 vols. (Oxford:

Oxford University Press, 2010); Simon Eliot and Jonathan Rose, eds., *A Companion to the History of the Book* (London: Blackwell, 2009); and David Finkelstein and Alistair McCleery, eds., *The Book History Reader*, 2nd ed. (New York: Routledge, 2006). There are individual national histories of the book for France, Great Britain, Germany, Ireland, Australia, the United States, Canada, and China.

7. For a notable exception, see the work of Lisa Gitelman, *Always Already New: Media, History and the Data of Culture* (Cambridge, MA: MIT Press, 2006), and her edited collection, *New Media, 1740–1915* (Cambridge, MA: MIT Press, 2003).

8. As recent neurological research suggests, when we read we simulate narrative situations in our brain by drawing on our past experiences in the world. Reading is made sense of through this translation between mental simulation and embodied experience. See Nicole K. Speer, Jeremy R. Reynolds, Khena M. Swallow, and Jeffrey M. Zacks, "Reading Stories Activates Neural Representations of Visual and Motor Experiences," *Psychological Science* 20, no. 8 (August 2009): 989–99. For recent work that has focused on the historical relationship between bodies and reading books, see Adrian Johns, "The Physiology of Reading: Print and the Passions," in *The Nature of the Book* (Chicago: University of Chicago Press, 1998), 380–443, and Karin Littau, *Theories of Reading: Books, Bodies and Bibliomania* (Cambridge: Polity, 2007). For work on bodies and digital reading, see Mark Hansen, *Bodies in Code* (New York: Routledge, 2006), and N. Katherine Hayles, *How We Became Posthuman: Virtual Bodies in Cybernetics, Literature, and Informatices* (Chicago: University of Chicago Press, 1999).

CHAPTER 1

1. Saint Augustine, *The Confessions*, trans. R. S. Pine-Coffin (New York: Penguin, 1961), 177.

2. Scholars estimate that it was around 300 AD when the codex achieved parity with the scroll. Colin H. Roberts and T. C. Skeat, *The Birth of the Codex* (London: British Academy, 1983), 75. On Christianity and reading, see Harry Y. Gamble, *Books and Readers in the Early Church: A History of Early Christian Texts* (New Haven, CT: Yale University Press, 1995), and Anthony Grafton and Megan Williams, *Christianity and the Transformation of the Book: Origen,*

Eusebius, and the Library of Caesarea (Cambridge, MA: Belknap Press, 2006).

3. David Katz, *The World of Touch*, ed. and trans. Lester E. Krueger (Hillsdale, NJ: LEA Publishers, 1989), 226. It was originally published in 1925 as *Der Aufbau der Tastwelt* (Leipzig: J. A. Barth, 1925). For a recent discussion of the relationship between the human hand and cognition, see Raymond Tallis, *The Hand: A Philosophical Inquiry into Human Being* (Edinburgh: Edinburgh University Press, 2003). One of the founding works in this field is André Leroi-Gourhan, *Gesture and Speech*, trans. Anna Bostock Berger (Cambridge, MA: MIT Press, 1993). Finally, for the argument that we have different neural pathways for our motor and visual relationship to words, see Stanislas Dehaene, *The Reading Brain: The Science and Evolution of a Human Invention* (New York: Viking, 2009), 57. According to neurologists, then, touch is a different cognitive means of knowing language.

4. *The Journal of Eugène Delacroix*, trans. Lucy Norton (Ithaca, NY: Cornell University Press, 1980), 29.

5. Michael Camille, "Seeing and Reading: Some Visual Implications of Medieval Literacy and Illiteracy," *Art History* 8, no. 1 (March 1985): 39; Horst Wenzel, "Von der Gotteshand zum Datenhandschuh. Zur Medialität des Begreifens," *Bild, Schrift, Zahl*, ed. Sybille Krämer and Horst Bredekamp (Munich: Fink, 2003), 25–55; Meyer Schapiro, *Words and Pictures: On the Literal and the Symbolic in the Illustration of a Text* (The Hague: Mouton, 1983).

6. John Bulwer, *Chirologia, or the Naturall Language of the Hand* (1644), n.p.

7. See the delightful introductory study by William H. Sherman, "Toward a History of the Manicule," *Used Books: Marking Readers in Renaissance England* (Philadelphia: Pennsylvania University Press, 2008), 25–52.

8. Claire Sherman, ed., *Writing on Hands: Memory and Knowledge in Early Modern Europe* (Seattle: University of Washington Press, 2000).

9. See useful catalogs such as *The Russian Avant-Garde Book, 1910–1934*, ed. Margit Rowell and Deborah Wye (New York: Museum of Modern Art, 2002); Renée Riese Hubert's *Surrealism and the Book* (Berkeley: University of California Press, 1988); and most recently,

Anna Sigridur Arnar, *The Book as Instrument: Stephane Mallarmé, the Artist's Book, and the Transformation of Print Culture* (Chicago: University of Chicago Press, 2011).

10. The clasp belongs to the history of elegant bindings, an important part of the story of the book's tactility. See Paul Needham, *Twelve Centuries of Bookbindings, 400–1600* (Oxford: Oxford University Press, 1979); D. Miner, *The History of Bookbinding, 525–1950* (Baltimore: Walters Art Gallery, 1957); and Philippa Marks, *Beautiful Bookbindings: A Thousand Years of the Bookbinder's Art* (Newcastle: Oak Knoll, 2011).

11. See Susan Tucker, Katherine Ott, and Patricia P. Buckler, eds., *The Scrapbook in American Life* (Philadelphia: Temple University Press, 2006), and Jessica Helfand, *Scrapbooks: An American History* (New Haven, CT: Yale University Press, 2008).

12. The practice of creating impressions from inked flowers (and not just pressing actual flowers in books) dates back at least to the Codex Atlanticus of Leonardo da Vinci. It became quite popular in the eighteenth century, for example, in the German botanist's Johann Hieronymus Kniphof's multivolume work *Botanica in Originali* (Erfurt: J. M. Funcke, 1747), which contained over one thousand impressions of plants. Auer's invention is discussed in his *Die Entdeckung des Naturselbstdruckes* (Vienna: K.k. Hof-u. Staatsdruckerei, 1854), which was written in four languages. For a brief history of the technique, see Roderick Cave and Geoffrey Wakeman, *Typographia Naturalis* (Wymondham: Brewhouse Press, 1967).

13. J. W. Goethe, *West-östlicher Divan*, in *Sämtliche Werke*, vol. 3.1, ed. Hendrik Birus (Frankfurt am Main: Deutscher Klassiker Verlag, 1994), 417.

14. While we often think in terms of small books becoming increasingly popular over time—that the book goes from large to small—there have always been small books. Indeed, much of the book's initial reception in competition with the scroll centered around its diminutive size. As the Roman poet Martial wrote in one of the earliest references to the codex, "Leave the great ones to their scrolls, a single hand can grasp me." Martial, *Epigrams*, ed. and trans. D. R. Shackleton Bailey, vol. 1 (Cambridge, MA: Harvard University Press, 1993), 43 (translation modified from the original).

15. Charles Nodier, "L'Amateur de livres," *Bulletin du Bibliophile*, no. 6

(June 1842): 249. See also the delightfully eclectic history of the topic, Holbrook Jackson, *The Anatomy of Bibliomania* (Urbana: University of Illinois Press, 2001).

16. Edgar Allan Poe, "Berenice," in *The Collected Works of Edgar Allen Poe*, ed. Thomas Ollive Mabbott, vol. 2 (Cambridge, MA: Belknap Press of Harvard University Press, 1978), 210.

17. See Noah Wardrip-Fruin et al., *Screen* (2002), in which you can bat around words with your hands; Marianne Schmidt, *Digitie* (2009), where you can wear a device that projects your hand onto a screen and allows you to interact with a remote person using the same device, a nice translation between the haptic and the visual; Chris O'Shea, *Hand from Above* (2009), a public installation that projects viewers onto a billboard being manipulated by a giant hand; Mark C. Marino, *A Show of Hands* (2007); Serge Bouchardon, Kevin Carpentiere, and Stéphanie Spenlé, *To Touch* (2009); and in particular, Serge Bouchardon and Vincent Volckaert, *Loss of Grasp* (2010), where the out of touchness of text provides a moving occasion to reflect on the triteness of language used in contemporary relationships.

18. This oceanic (as opposed to terrestrial) nature of digital textuality has been nicely rendered in Nick Montfort and Stephanie Strickland's *Sea and Spar Between* (2011), which algorithmically combines the writings of Melville and Dickinson to produce as many stanzas as there are fish in the sea (about 225 trillion). As you pass over them with the cursor, the lines of verse writhe, wiggle, and shift like marine life. http://www.saic.edu/webspaces/portal/degrees_resources/departments/writing/DNSP11_SeaandSparBetween/index.html. For the classic example of an intentionally disappearing digital text, see William Gibson's *Agrippa (A Book of the Dead)* (1992), which was designed to become unreadable after a single use.

19. For a discussion on the nature of the materiality of digital texts, see Matthew Kirschenbaum's prize-winning study, *Mechanisms: New Media and the Forensic Imagination* (Cambridge, MA: MIT Press, 2008). To give just one example of the complexity of digital text's thereness, in order to make the opening line of Faust's famous monologue legible on a standard web browser would require something like the equivalent of 8,062 lines of code. The question that the bibliographer F. W. Bateson once famously asked, "If the *Mona Lisa* is in the Louvre, where is *Hamlet*?" has only gotten more complicated today.

20. Shelley Jackson, "Eyelid," *My Body—A Wunderkammer* (1997),

http://collection.eliterature.org/1/works/jackson__my_body_a_
wunderkammer/eyelid.html. This might also be one reason digital
texts bluster so often about the body as a form of compensation.
As Alan Sondheim writes in *Internet Text*, "Spread your lips, smell
your hands. Finger your ass, smell your fingers. Squeeze your balls,
smell your hands. Squeeze your cock, smell your fingers. Would you
be my animal." http://collection.eliterature.org/1/works/sondheim__
internet_text.html.

21. For new research in haptic computing, see the work of the MIT Touch
Lab and the UBC Human Communication Technologies Lab, among
others. For a discussion of the historical relationship between touch
and technology, see Mark Paterson, *The Senses of Touch: Haptics,
Affects and Technologies* (New York: Berg, 2007). On "handheld
culture," see Byron Hawk, David M. Rieder, and Ollie Oviedo, eds.,
Small Tech: The Culture of Digital Tools (Minneapolis: University of
Minnesota Press, 2008). This renewed attention to design and interactivity is often denoted as a "material turn" in computing studies,
distinguishing itself from older concerns about virtuality and simulation. See Erica Robles and Mikael Wiberg, "Texturing the 'Material
Turn' in Interaction Design," *Proceedings of the Fourth International
Conference on Tangible Embedded and Embodied Interaction TEI
'10* (New York: AMC Press, 2010), 137–44.

22. On the history of the button, see Finn Brunton, "The Single Abrupt
Movement: Gesture, Interface, Mechanization" (forthcoming).

23. Roland Barthes, *The Pleasure of the Text*, trans. Richard Miller (New
York: Hill and Wang, 1975), 41.

24. For a discussion of online forums where computer programmers talk
about their pain, see Michele White, *The Body and the Screen*, 186.
For a discussion of "text neck," see http://text-neck.com/. As the Text
Next Institute writes on its website: "Medical research has shown
that long term forward head posture will cause early spinal arthritis,
disc degeneration, headaches, up to a 30% decrease in lung capacity
to just name a few conditions. A survey was conducted with 6,000
chronic headache sufferers and the only common finding among
them was the loss or reversal of the normal curve in the neck."

25. In the new Alice for iPad reading interface, when you shake the iPad
it "unlocks" secret passageways through the text. It replaces a mental operation—who hasn't created their own subterranean passage
through a book?—with a physically determinate one.

26. As numerous critics have pointed out, the mind is freer when not following the constrained pathways of hypertext. What interests me is the way corporal *activity* is repeatedly posited as a solution to the inactivity of reading. We fear reading's inaction, a point that could be tied to a larger anxiety about the place of the humanities today, a field of knowledge that depends heavily on the inertia of reading. In this sense, the humanities lack "action" and thus "impact." For a critique of the myth of interactivity, see Marjorie Perloff, "Digital Poetics and Differential Text," *New Media Poetics: Contexts, Technotexts, and Theories*, ed. Adelaide Morris and Thomas Swiss (Cambridge, MA: MIT Press, 2006), 143–64.

27. Mark Bauerlein, "Online Literacy Is a Lesser Kind," *Chronicle of Higher Education*, September 19, 2008, http://chronicle.com/article/ Online-Literacy-Is-a-Lesser/28307.

28. For a more extensive discussion of Morrissey and for an indispensable introduction to the canon of electronic literature, see N. Katherine Hayles's anthology, *Electronic Literature: New Horizons for the Literary* (Notre Dame, IN: University of Notre Dame Ward-Phillips, 2008).

29. Matthew Kirschenbaum, *Mechanisms*, 26.

30. In December 2009, the Bush administration claimed to have "lost" 22 million e-mails. "You can't erase e-mails, not today," Senator Patrick Leahy remarked during a passionate speech from the Senate floor. "They've gone through too many servers. Those e-mails are there—they just don't want to produce them. It's like the infamous 18-minute gap in the Nixon White House tapes." Leahy's comparison to the Nixon "tapes" was not only good political theater. It was also an insightful comment about the historical dynamic of the lost and found of information. That we had been here before with tapes, and not servers, was an example of something recurrent, something that extends deep into the bibliographic record. See Pete Yost, "22 Million Missing Bush White House Emails Found," *Associated Press*, December 14, 2009.

31. For research into questions of digital preservation, see Matthew Kirschenbaum, "Approaches to Managing and Collecting Born-Digital Literary Materials for Scholarly Use," NEH Whitepaper (2008), http://www.neh.gov/ODH/Default.aspx?tabid=111&id=37; the numerous articles in the *International Journal of Digital Curation*; and the ongoing work of the Open Planets Foundation.

32. Plato, *Phaedrus*, trans. Alexander Nehamas and Paul Woodruff (Indianapolis: Hackett, 1995), 81.

33. The origin of the bedtime story as both a widespread practice and a genre of writing dates back to the 1870s. See Patricia Crain, "Bedtime Stories," *Reading: Selected Essays from the English Institute*, ed. Joseph Slaughter (Cambridge, MA: English Institute in Collaboration with the American Council of Learned Societies, forthcoming). For a discussion of the relationship between sleep and reading, see Seth Lerer, "Epilogue: Falling Asleep over the History of the Book," *PMLA* 121, no. 1 (2006): 229–34. For a discussion of the historical convergence of reading and dreaming, see Andrew Piper, *Dreaming in Books: The Making of the Bibliographic Imagination in the Romantic Age* (Chicago: University of Chicago Press, 2009), 1–17.

34. Walt Whitman, *Leaves of Grass and Other Writings*, ed. Michael Moon (New York: Norton, 2002), 13.

35. As researcher Kalina Christoff has argued, the mind is not only *more* active when it wanders, but it does so in a more associative way than during focused cognition. "Although it may undermine our immediate goals," writes Christoff, "mind wandering may enable the parallel operation of diverse brain areas in the service of distal goals that extend beyond the current task." Kalina Christoff et al., "Experience Sampling during fMRI Reveals Default Network and Executive System Contributions to Mind Wandering," *Proceedings of the National Academy of Sciences* 106, no. 21 (2009): 8719–24, and J. W. Schooler et al., "Meta-Awareness, Perceptual Decoupling, and the Wandering Mind," *Trends in Cognitive Sciences* 15, no. 7 (2011): 319–26.

CHAPTER 2

1. Honoré de Balzac, *The Unknown Masterpiece*, trans. Richard Howard (New York: New York Review of Books, 2001), 40.

2. On the relationship between looking and reading, see Garrett Stewart, *The Look of Reading: Book, Painting, Text* (Chicago: University of Chicago Press, 2006), and *Bookwork: Medium to Object to Concept to Art* (Chicago: University of Chicago Press, 2011); Stanislas Dehaene, *Reading in the Brain* (New York: Viking, 2009), 122–42; and Mark Changizi, *The Vision Revolution* (Dallas: Benbella Books, 2009), 163–210.

3. Authorial portraits in books date back at least to the oldest extant manuscript of Virgil from the Vergilius Romanus manuscript in the Vatican library of the late fifth century AD. The earliest print authorial frontispiece is thought to be Aesopus, *Vita et Fabulae* (Strasbourg: Heinrich Knoblochtzer, [1485?]), although like its manuscript predecessors it lacks any resemblance to the art of portraiture that would come to dominate frontispieces in the seventeenth century. See David Piper, *The Image of the Poet: British Poets and their Portraits* (Oxford: Clarendon, 1982); Ruth Mortimer, *A Portrait of the Author in Sixteenth-Century France* (Chapel Hill, NC: Hanes Foundation, 1980); and Margaret M. Smoth, *The Title Page: Its Early Development, 1460–1510* (New Castle, DE: Oak Knoll, 2000) 79, 88.

4. For a discussion of Byron, portraiture, and the birth of celebrity culture, see Tom Mole, *Byron's Romantic Celebrity: Industrial Culture and the Hermeneutic of Intimacy* (New York: Palgrave Macmillan, 2007). For a discussion of the role of the portrait in Balzac, see Isabelle Mimouni, *Balzac illusionniste: Les arts dans l'oeuvre de l'écrivain* (Paris: Adam Biro, 1999), 26–53.

5. Andrew Keen, *The Sunday Edition*, CBC Radio, July 15, 2007.

6. *The Odes of Pindar*, vol. 1, trans. Peter Edmund Laurent (Oxford: Munday and Slatter, 1824), 40.

7. For a discussion of the visual acquisition of letters, see Stanislas Dehaene, *Reading in the Brain*, 137–42, 172–93, and Mark Changizi, *The Vision Revolution*, 163–210. It should be noted that after an initial neurological overlap between the visual acquisition of letters and faces, these objects are processed in slightly separate regions of the brain. They may be processually similar, but their handling ultimately occupies different spaces of the brain's geography.

8. For a discussion of the political consequences of physiognomic thought, see Richard T. Gray, *About Face: German Physiognomic Thought from Lavater to Auschwitz* (Detroit: Wayne State University Press, 2004).

9. Johann Caspar Lavater, *Physiognomische Fragmente*, ed. Christoph Siegrist (Stuttgart: Reclam, 1984), 152.

10. See Hans Blumenberg's classic study *The Legibility of the World* (Chicago: University of Chicago Press, 1990). For a discussion of the way writing changed visual knowledge from writing's inception in the third millennium BC, see Denise Schmandt-Besserat, who writes, "In the literate period, reading images becomes akin to reading texts."

When Writing Met Art: From Symbol to Story (Austin: University of Texas Press, 2007), 25.

11. Paul Valéry, "My Faust," in *The Collected Works of Paul Valéry*, vol. 3, *Plays*, trans. D. Paul and R. Fitzgerald (Princeton, NJ: Princeton University Press, 1971), 32.

12. On intersections between the history of photography and the book, see Carol Armstrong, *Scenes in a Library: Reading the Photograph in the Book, 1843–1875* (Cambridge, MA: MIT Press, 1998); Peggy Ann Kusnerz, ed., "Special Issue: Photography and the Book," *History of Photography* 26, no. 3 (2002); Andrew Roth, *The Open Book: A History of the Photographic Book from 1878 to the Present* (Göteborg: Hasselblad Center, 2004); Martin Parr and Gerry Badger, eds., *The Photobook: A History*, 2 vols. (London: Phaidon, 2004); and François Brunet, "Photography and the Book," *Photography and Literature* (London: Reaktion, 2009), 35–62.

13. Cited in Julian Cox and Colid Ford, *Julia Margaret Cameron: The Complete Photographs* (Los Angeles: Getty Publications, 2003), 66.

14. Andrew Piper, "Transitional Figures: Image, Translation and the Ballad from Broadside to Photography," *Book Illustration in the Long Eighteenth Century: Reconfiguring the Visual Periphery of the Text*, ed. Christina Ionescu (Cambridge: Cambridge Scholars Publishing, 2011), 157–91.

15. Eudora Welty, "A Sweet Devouring," in *The Eye of the Story: Selected Essays and Reviews* (New York: Random House, 1977), 280.

16. For a discussion of the aesthetics of the webcam, see Michele White, *The Body and the Screen: Theories of Internet Spectatorship* (Cambridge, MA: MIT Press, 2006), 57–84. For a review of the new aesthetics of portraiture, see William A. Ewing, *Face: The New Photographic Portrait* (London: Thames and Hudson, 2006).

17. Walter Benjamin, "Little History of Photography," in *The Work of Art in the Age of Its Technological Reproducibility and Other Writings on Media* (Cambridge, MA: Belknap Press of Harvard University Press, 2008).

18. Ellen Ullman, *Close to the Machine: Technophilia and Its Discontents* (San Francisco: City Lights, 1997), 3.

19. Naomi S. Baron, *Always On: Language in an Online and Mobile World* (Oxford: Oxford University Press, 2008).

20. Robert Darnton, *The Forbidden Bestsellers of Pre-Revolutionary France*, (New York: W. W. Norton, 1995).

21. One definition of pornography is that it is comprised of a set of visual practices whose primary aim is to conflate the sensory experiences of site and touch. In this, there is a correlation between the type of close looking that the web promotes and the type of content that is its most prevalent visual material. Commentators remark often enough on the importance of pornography to the development of the web. But would it be going too far to say that the kind of close looking that the web promotes is always in a sense veering towards the pornographic? For a useful discussion of the problematic art-historical distinctions between "art" and "pornography," see Kelly Dennis, *Art/Porn* (New York and Oxford: Berg, 2009).

22. Walter Benjamin, "Convolute N," in *The Arcades Project*, trans. Howard Eiland and Kevin McLaughlin (Cambridge, MA: Belknap Press of Harvard University Press, 1999), 456–89, 458.

23. Hermann Broch, *The Sleepwalkers*, trans. Willa and Edwin Muir (New York: Vintage, 1996), 376 (modified from the original). For a contemporary update of the idea, see Doug Aitken's *Sleepwalkers* (2007), which was shown as an outdoor exhibition at the New York Museum of Modern Art.

24. First, to clarify some terms: a 419 letter is the e-mail you receive almost daily in your in-box asking you for money ("Dear Sir . . ."). The sock puppet is a fake persona created for social networking sites to promote products but also for the purposes of military surveillance. With the invention of three-dimensional printing, researchers have now begun to experiment with printing cells and replacement organic tissue for the body. On the complicated distinctions between human and machine communication, see Brian Christian, *The Most Human Human: What Talking with Computers Teaches Us about What It Means to Be Alive* (New York: Doubleday, 2011), 9. On the zombie as the new icon of modern life, see the inspired piece by Chuck Klostermann, "My Zombie, Myself: Why Modern Life Feels Rather Undead," *New York Times*, December 3, 2010, http://www.nytimes .com/2010/12/05/arts/television/05zombies.html. For a discussion of the vast amount of organic waste being manufactured in the biological sciences today that is technically "alive" but not afforded the same rights as living "beings," see Thierry Bardini, *Junkware* (Minneapolis: University of Minnesota Press, 2011), 23.

25. Talan Memmott, "Delimited Meshings," *Cauldron and Net* 3 (Spring

2001): http://www.studiocleo.com/cauldron/volume3/index.html. For a discussion of the way Facebook moves us from a social model based around groups to one comprised of "egocentric networks," see Danah Boyd, "Friends, Friendsters, and Top 8: Writing Community into Being on Social Networking Sites," *First Monday* 11, no. 12 (2006): http://firstmonday.org/htbin/cgiwrap/bin/ojs/index.php/fm/article/view/1418/1336.

26. On the history of the "optical unconscious," which is a term that derives from the work of Walter Benjamin, and the centrality of the graph to modern art, see Rosalind Krauss, *The Optical Unconscious* (Cambridge, MA: MIT Press, 1993).

27. For a review of the issues, see Susan B. Barnes "A Privacy Paradox: Social Networking in the United States," *First Monday* 11, no. 9 (2006); Anders Albrechtslund, "Online Social Networking as Participatory Surveillance," *First Monday* 13, no. 3 (2008); and James Grimmelmann, "The Privacy Virus," in *Facebook and Philosophy*, ed. D. E. Wittkower (Chicago: Open Court, 2010), 3–13. In response to the pervasive surveillance of digital media, there is a host of new critical work on techniques of *sousveillance*, practices of observing digital surveillance. See Steve Mann and Robert Guerra, "The Witnessential Net," *Proceedings of IEEE International Symposium on Wearable Computing* (2001): 47–54, and Jason Nolan, Steve Mann, and Barry Wellman, "Sousveillance: Wearable and Digital Tools in Surveilled Environments," in *Small Tech: The Culture of Digital Tools*, ed. Byron Hawk, David M. Rieder, and Ollie Oviedo (Minneapolis: University of Minnesota Press, 2008), 179–96.

28. Don DeLillo, *Valparaiso* (New York: Scribner, 2003), 25. For a history of the emergence of privacy, see Patricia Meyer Spacks, *Privacy: Concealing the Eighteenth-Century Self* (Chicago: University of Chicago Press, 2003). For current reflections on the withdrawal of privacy from contemporary life, see Jeffrey Rosen, "The Web Means the End of Forgetting," *New York Times Magazine*, July 15, 2010, and Harry Blatterer, Pauline Johnson, and Maria Markus, eds. *Modern Privacy: Shifting Boundaries, New Forms* (Basingstoke: Palgrave, 2010).

29. This work counts as its spiritual forerunners not only that of Cameron, but also Lee Friedlander's collection of interrupted self-images in *Self-Portrait* (New York: Haywire Press, 1970) and his collection

of photographs of television screens in *Little Screens* (San Francisco: Fraenkel Gallery, 2001). See also the role that pixelation and the photographic blur play more recently in the photographs of Thomas Ruff and the photo-realist paintings of Gerhard Richter.

30. This is what the German Enlightenment philosopher G. E. Lessing meant by the animal's *Bestandheit* in his treatise on the fable—from the verb *stehen*, "to stand." See Gotthold Ephraim Lessing, "Von dem Gebrauch der Tiere in der Fabel," in *Fabeln*, ed. Heinz Rölleke (Stuttgart: Reclam, 1967), 110. For a recent general history of children's literature, see Seth Lerer, *Children's Literature: A Reader's History, from Aesop to Harry Potter* (Chicago: University of Chicago Press, 2008).

31. Paula Modersohn-Becker, *Letters and Journals*, ed. G. Busch and L. von Reinken (Evanston, IL: Northwestern University Press, 1998), 270.

32. For a discussion of the role that the face plays in the ethical practice of "acknowledgment" (*Anerkennung* in German), see Axel Honneth, "Invisibility: On the Epistemology of Recognition," *Aristotelian Society Supplementary* 75, no. 1 (2003): 111–26. See his foundational work in German, Axel Honneth, *Kampf um Anerkennung: Zur moralischen Grammatik sozialer Konflikte* (Frankfurt am Main: Suhrkamp, 1993); and in English, Nancy Fraser and Axel Honneth, *Redistribution or Recognition? A Political-Philosophical Exchange* (London: Verso, 2003).

CHAPTER 3

1. Pliny the Younger, *Letters*, vol. 2, trans. William Melmoth (Cambridge, MA: Harvard University Press, 1961), 27.

2. John Keats, *Letters*, 4th ed., ed. Maurice Buxton Forman (London: Oxford University Press, 1952), 101.

3. Erasmus, *Collected Works*, vol. 10, trans. R. A. B Mynors and Alexander Dalzell (Toronto: University of Toronto Press, 1992), 74. Erasmus was echoing the well-known biblical trope of eating God's word in Ezekiel 2:9–10.

4. John Miedema, *Slow Reading* (Duluth, MN: Litwin Books, 2009).

5. Evelyn B. Tribble, *Margins and Marginality: The Printed Page in Early Modern England* (Charlottesville: University of Virginia Press, 1993).

6. Virginia Woolf, *To the Lighthouse*, ed. Stella McNichol (London: Penguin, 2000), 129.

7. Susan Orlean, *The Orchid Thief* (New York: Ballantine, 2000), 109.

8. Paul Saenger, *Space between Words: The Origins of Silent Reading* (Stanford, CA: Stanford University Press, 1997).

9. Honoré de Balzac, *The Wild Ass's Skin*, trans. Herbert J. Hunt (London: Penguin, 1977), 22.

10. For the argument that the codex is fundamentally about a nonlinear access to reading, see Peter Stallybrass, "Books and Scrolls: Navigating the Bible," in *Books and Readers in Early Modern England*, ed. Jennifer Andersen and Elizabeth Sauer (Philadelphia: University of Pennsylvania Press, 2002), 42–79.

11. Marjorie Garber, " " " (Quotation Marks)," *Critical Inquiry* 25, no. 4 (1999): 653–79.

12. Garrett Stewart, *The Look of Reading* (Chicago: University of Chicago Press, 2006), 131.

13. J. W. Goethe, *Begegnungen und Gespräche*, ed. Renate Grumach (Berlin: de Gruyter, 1999), 2414.

14. André Leroi-Gourhan, *Gesture and Speech*, trans. Anna Bostock Berger (Cambridge, MA: MIT Press, 1993).

15. As Lev Manovich writes, "Regardless of whether new media objects present themselves as linear narratives, interactive narratives, databases or something else, underneath, on the level of material organization, they are all databases." Lev Manovich, *Language of New Media* (Cambridge, MA: MIT Press, 2001), 228. For this reason Alan Liu calls the digital interface a "data pour," the result of a "query" of structured language that resides elsewhere. Alan Liu, "Transcendental Data: Toward a Cultural History and Aesthetics of the New Encoded Discourse," *Critical Inquiry* 31, no. 1 (2004): 49–84. N. Katherine Hayles employed early on the productive notion of the "flickering signifier" to describe the impermanence of digital text. See *How We Became Posthuman: Virtual Bodies in Cybernetics, Literature and Informatics* (Chicago: Chicago University Press, 1999), 25–49.

16. Craig Mod, "Books in the Age of the iPad," March 2010, http://craigmod.com/journal/ipad_and_books/. Every age needs its French philosophers, and the work of Gilles Deleuze and Félix Guattari, especially their work on the "plateau," seems to have become a new

point of reference for our contemporary moment. For a primer, see Gilles Deleuze and Félix Guattari, *A Thousand Plateaus*, trans. Brian Massumi (Minneapolis: University of Minnesota Press, 1987).

17. For an introduction to satellite culture, see Lisa Parks, *Cultures in Orbit: Satellites and the Televisual* (Durham, NC: Duke University Press, 2005).

18. For John Cayley, this new three-dimensionality of writing owes much of its origins to the mobilization of writing *in time* through the medium of the film credit sequence. Cayley's insight is interesting for how it draws attention to the way other media like film are important, and often overlooked, influences on the development of reading. John Cayley, "Writing on Complex Surfaces," *Dichtung Digital* 35 (2005): http://www.dichtung-digital.org/2005/2-Cayley.htm.

19. "The iPad in the Eyes of the Digerati," *New York Times*, April 6, 2010, http://roomfordebate.blogs.nytimes.com/2010/04/06/the-ipad-in-the-eyes-of-the-digerati/.

20. Emily Dickinson, *The Complete Poems*, ed. Thomas H. Johnson (New York: Little Brown, 1961), 506.

21. See in particular the work of Sara Cordes and Rochel Gelman, "The Young Numerical Mind: When Does It Count?," in *Handbook of Mathematical Cognition*, ed. Jamie I. D. Campbell (New York: Psychology Press, 2005), 128–42, and Stanislas Dehaene, *The Number Sense: How the Mind Creates Mathematics* (Oxford: Oxford University Press, 2011).

22. Friedrich Nietzsche, *Unfashionable Observations*, trans. Richard T. Gray (Stanford, CA: Stanford University Press, 1995), 192.

23. J. W. Goethe, *The Man of Fifty*, trans. Andrew Piper (London: Hesperus Press, 2004), 13.

CHAPTER 4

1. Ernst Robert Curtius, "Goethe as Administrator," in *Essays on European Literature*, trans. Michael Kowal (Princeton, NJ: Princeton University Press, 1973), 58–72.

2. For Goethe's note, see Goethe- und Schiller-Archiv 25/W2002; for Melville, see http://www.boisestate.edu/melville/popup.asp?fn=17.

3. For the argument about the importance of handwriting for print, see Peter Stallybrass, *Printing for Manuscript* (Philadelphia: University of Pennsylvania Press, forthcoming). For a historical discussion of

the relationship between handwriting and print, see Roger Chartier, "Le manuscrit à l'âge de l'imprimé (XVe–XVIIIe siècles)," *La lettre clandestine* 7 (1998): 175–93. For a discussion of the role of handwriting in generating sentimental networks of readers in the nineteenth century, see Andrew Piper, *Dreaming in Books: The Making of the Bibliographic Imagination in the Romantic Age* (Chicago: University of Chicago Press), 121–52. And for a discussion of the way more printed books gave rise to more letter writing about books, see Catherine J. Golden, *Posting It: The Victorian Revolution in Letter Writing* (Gainesville: University Press of Florida, 2009).

4. Roland Barthes, *Mourning Diary* (New York: Hill and Wang, 2010), 17.

5. Recorded on October 28, 1889. Walt Whitman, *Daybooks and Notebooks*, in *The Collected Writings of Walt Whitman*, vol. 2, ed. William White, Gay Wilson Allen, and Sculley Bradley (New York: New York University Press, 1978), 539.

6. See Box 123, Folder 8 and Box 124, Folder 10, Susan Sontag Archive, Department of Special Collections, Charles E. Young Research Library, University of California, Los Angeles.

7. Stephen Kuusisto, Deborah Tall, and David Weiss, eds., *The Poet's Notebook* (New York: W. W. Norton, 1995), 190.

8. Stephen Kuusisto, Deborah Tall, and David Weiss, *The Poet's Notebook*, 224.

9. Stendhal, *The Life of Henry Brulard*, trans. John Sturrock (New York: New York Review Books, 2004), 311.

10. James Joyce, *The Finnegans Wake Notebooks at Buffalo*, ed. Vincent Deane, Daniel Ferrer, and Geert Lernout (Turnhout: Brepols, 2004), VI.B.47.016, VI.B.47.025, VI.B.47.043.

11. William Hopkins's *The Flying Pen-Man, or The Art of Short Writing* (London, 1674), n.p.

12. Stendhal, *The Life of Henry Brulard*, 37.

13. Samuel Taylor Coleridge, *The Notebooks of Samuel Taylor Coleridge*, vol. 1, ed. Kathleen Coburn (London: Routledge, 1957), §1554.

14. J. W. Goethe, *Maxims and Reflections*, trans. Elizabeth Stopp (London: Penguin, 1998), 21.

15. As Ann Blair reminds us, many premodern note-taking devices were designed to be erasable, from wax tablets to sand trays to slate boards even to treated paper that could be easily erased. See Ann Blair, "Note-Taking as Information Management," in *Too Much*

to Know: Managing Scholarly Information before the Modern Age (New Haven, CT: Yale University Press, 2010).

16. E. A. Poe, "Marginalia," *Democratic Review* 14 (November 1844): 484, emphasis in original. Or as Poe would later write in the same article, "Just as the goodness of your true pun is in the direct ratio of its intolerability, so is nonsense the essential sense of the Marginal Note" (485).

17. Samuel Taylor Coleridge, *Notebooks*, vol. 2.1, ed. Kathleen Coburn (London: Routledge and Kegan Paul, 1962), §2406.

18. Georg Lichtenberg, *The Waste Books*, trans. and ed. R. J. Hollingdale (New York: New York Review Books), 100.

19. Walt Whitman, *Notebooks and Unpublished Prose Manuscripts*, in *The Collected Writings of Walt Whitman*, vol. 1, ed. Edward Grier (New York: New York University Press, 1984), 230.

20. Achim von Arnim, Goethe- und Schiller-Archiv 03/339 Bl. 13 Rs.

21. Matthew J. Burccoli, *The Notebooks of F. Scott Fitzgerald* (New York: Harcourt Brace Jovanovich, 1978), 18.

22. See Ann Moss, *Printed Commonplace-Books and the Structuring of Renaissance Thought* (Oxford: Clarendon Press, 1996), and Ann Blair, "Note-Taking as Information Management."

23. Cited in Ann Moss, *Printed Commonplace-Books*, 121.

24. William H. Sherman, *Used Books: Marking Readers in Renaissance England* (Philadelphia: University of Pennsylvania Press, 2008); H. J. Jackson, *Marginalia: Readers Writing in Books* (New Haven, CT: Yale University Press, 2001); and Anthony Grafton, "Is the History of Reading a Marginal Enterprise?," *Papers of the Bibliographical Society of America* 91 (1997): 139–57.

25. Brenda R. Silver, *Virginia Woolf's Reading Notebooks* (Princeton, NJ: Princeton University Press, 1983), 157.

26. Leah Price, "Reading: The State of the Discipline," *Book History* 7 (2004): 313.

27. Melville's edition of Dante is discussed in Piero Boitani, "Moby-Dante," *Dante for a New Millennium*, ed. Teodolinda Barolini and Wayne Storey (New York: Fordham University Press, 2003) 435–50.

28. Hermann Melville, *Pierre: Or, The Ambiguities*, in *The Writings of Hermann Melville*, vol. 7 (Evanston, IL: Northwestern University Press, 1971), 251.

29. For a few samples in the popular press, see Ann Wroe, "Handwrit-

ing: An Elegy," *More Intelligent Life* (November/December 2011): http://moreintelligentlife.com/content/ideas/ann-wroe/handwriting-elegy?page=full; Graham T. Beck, "Tempest in an Inkpot," *Morning News*, August 31, 2011: http://moreintelligentlife.com/content/ideas/ann-wroe/handwriting-elegy?page=full; and Kitty Florey, *Script and Scribble: The Rise and Fall of Handwriting* (New York: Melville House, 2009). On the scholarly side, see the work coming out of the field of "graphonomics" that studies the relationship between drawing and handwriting and its cognitive effects: http://www.graphonomics.org/.

30. Anne Trubek, "Stop Teaching Handwriting," *Good*, February 11, 2008, http://www.good.is/post/stop-teaching-handwriting/.

31. As Steve Graham has argued, "Handwriting may require so much effort for some young writers that they develop an approach to composing that minimizes the use of other writing processes, such as planning and revising, because they exert considerable processing demands as well." S. Graham, K. Harris, and B. Fink, "Is Handwriting Causally Related to Learning to Write?," *Journal of Educational Psychology* 92, no. 4 (2000): 620. See Steve Graham, "Want to Improve Children's Writing? Don't Neglect Their Handwriting," *Education Digest* 76, no. 1 (September 2010): 49–55; V. Berninger and S. Graham, "Language by Hand: A Synthesis of a Decade of Research in Handwriting," *Handwriting Review* 12 (1998): 11–25; and S. Graham and N. Weintraub, "A Review of Handwriting Research," *Educational Psychology Review* 8 (1996): 7–87.

32. Ray Nash, *American Penmanship, 1800–1850* (Worcester, MA: American Antiquarian Society, 1969). See also Mary Carruthers, who reminds us of the physicality of writing with one's hand in the Middle Ages when the dominant writing surface was animal's skin. "One must break it, rough it up, 'wound' it in some way with a sharply pointed instrument. Erasure involved roughing up the physical surface even more…[including] pumice stones and other scrapers." Mary Carruthers, *The Craft of Thought: Meditation, Rhetoric and the Making of Images, 400–1200* (Cambridge: Cambridge University Press, 1998), 102.

33. Fotini Bonoti, "Writing and Drawing Performance of School Age Children: Is There Any Relationship?," *School Psychology International* 26 (2005): 243–54.

34. Steven Johnson, "The Glass Box and the Commonplace Book," lec-

ture delivered at Columbia University, April 23, 2010, http://www
.stevenberlinjohnson.com/2010/04/the-glass-box-and-the-common-
place-book.html.

35. Erasmus, *Ciceronianus*, in *Collected Works*, vol. 28, trans. Betty I.
Knott (Toronto: University of Toronto Press, 1986), 402. On the
history of the reader as a bee, see Matthew Brown, *The Pilgrim and
the Bee: Reading Rituals and Book Culture in Early New England*
(Philadelphia: University of Pennsylvania Press, 2007). On the importance of copying to human culture, see Marcus Boon, *In Praise
of Copying* (Cambridge, MA: Harvard University Press, 2010).

36. Edith Norris et al., "Children's Use of Drawing as a Pre-Writing
Strategy," *Journal of Research in Reading* 21, no. 1 (1998): 69–74.

37. Denise Schmandt-Besserat, *When Writing Met Art: From Symbol to
Story* (Austin: University of Texas Press, 2007).

38. Linda Hermer-Vazquez, Elizabeth S. Spelke, and Alla S. Katsnelson,
"Sources of Flexibility in Human Cognition: Dual-Task Studies of
Space and Language," *Cognitive Psychology* 39 (1999): 3–36. This is
discussed in a wider developmental context in Charles Fernyhough, *A
Thousand Days of Wonder: A Scientist's Chronicle of His Daughter's
Developing Mind* (New York: Avery, 2009).

39. For examples of new digital authorial archives, see the Walt Whitman Archive (www.whitmanarchive.org/), the William Blake Archive
(www.blakearchive.org/blake/), the Rosetti Archive (www.rossetti
archive.org/), and the Poetess Archive (www.poetessarchive.com/).
For a discussion of the history of the "document," see the work in
progress by Lisa Gitelman.

40. Ralph Waldo Emerson, "Friendship," in *The Collected Works*, vol. 2,
ed. Alfred R. Ferguson and Jean Ferguson Carr (Cambridge, MA:
Belknap Press, 1979), 116.

41. Walter Benjamin, *Selected Writings*, vol. 1, ed. Marcus Bullock and
Michael W. Jennings (Cambridge, MA: Belknap Press, 1996), 456.

CHAPTER 5

1. Chris Anderson, *Free: The Future of a Radical Price* (New York:
Hyperion, 2009); David Kelty, *Two Bits: The Cultural Significance
of Free Software* (Durham, NC: Duke University Press, 2008).

2. As Stephen Nissenbaum writes, "Books were on the cutting edge of

a commercial Christmas, making up more than half of the earliest items advertised as Christmas gifts." Stephen Nissenbaum, *The Battle for Christmas* (New York: Vintage, 1997), 140.

3. *Gaben der Milde: Für die Bücher-Verloosung zum Vortheil hülfloser Krieger* (Berlin, 1817–18), and *The Queen's Gift Book: In Aid of Queen Mary's Convalescent Auxiliary Hospitals for Soldiers and Sailors Who Have Lost Their Limbs in the War* (London: Hodder and Stoughton, 1918).

4. The literature on this subject is massive and growing. For the history of copyright, see Martha Woodmansee, *The Author, Art, and the Market: Rereading the History of Aesthetics* (New York: Columbia University Press, 1994), and Mark Rose, *Authors and Owners: The Invention of Copyright* (Cambridge, MA: Harvard University Press, 1993). For critiques of contemporary copyright legislation, see Siva Vaidhyanathan, *Copyrights and Copywrongs: The Rise of Intellectual Property and How It Threatens Creativity* (New York: New York University Press, 2003); Lawrence Lessig, *Free Culture: How Big Media Uses Technology and the Law to Lock Down Culture and Control Creativity* (New York: Penguin Press, 2004); Lewis Hyde, *Common as Air: Revolution, Art, and Ownership* (New York: Farrar, Strauss, and Giroux, 2010); and Tarleton Gillespie, *Wired Shut: Copyright and the Shape of Digital Culture* (Cambridge, MA: MIT Press, 2007).

5. Natalie Zemon Davis, "Beyond the Market: Books as Gifts in Sixteenth-Century France," *Transactions of the Royal Historical Society* 5, no. 33 (1983): 69.

6. Not surprisingly, with the recent overproliferation of reading material there has been a rise of theoretical reflections on the problem of commonality. See Roberto Esposito, *Communitas: The Origin and Destiny of Community*, trans. Timothy Campbell (Stanford, CA: Stanford University Press, 2010); Michael Hardt and Antonio Negri, *Commonwealth* (Cambridge, MA: Belknap Press, 2009); and Giorgio Agamben, *The Coming Community*, trans. Michael Hardt (Minneapolis: University of Minnesota Press, 1993).

7. The classic treatment on the history of gift-giving practices is Marcel Mauss, *The Gift*, trans. W. D. Halls (New York: Norton, 2000). Mauss was fascinated by the way gifts were very often part of larger circuits of exchange, that every gift implied an obligation to give

something back. In my focus on sharing as one type of giving, I'm interested more in the problems of co-ownership and commonality that attend the circulation of objects, not in the form of something that needs to be returned at a later date, but that which might be held in common simultaneously. What are the practices and technologies that have allowed us in the past to overcome the temporality of giving to have something more spiritual or intellectual in common?

8. Clara Gebert, ed., *An Anthology of Elizabethan Dedications and Prefaces* (New York: Russell and Russell, 1933), 107.

9. Kathy Eden, *Friends Hold All Things in Common: Tradition, Intellectual Property, and the Adages of Erasmus* (New Haven, CT: Yale University Press, 2001).

10. James Johnston, ed., *The Alba Amicorum of George Strachan, George Craig, Thomas Cumming* (Aberdeen: University of Aberdeen, 1924).

11. Ralph Waldo Emerson, "Friendship," in *The Collected Works*, vol. 2, ed. Alfred R. Ferguson and Jean Ferguson Carr (Cambridge, MA: Belknap Press, 1979), 120.

12. Andrew Piper, *Dreaming in Books: The Making of the Bibliographic Imagination in the Romantic Age* (Chicago: University of Chicago Press), 121–52.

13. Markman Ellis, *The Coffee-House: A Cultural History* (London: Weidenfeld and Nicolson, 2004), 187. See also Brian Cowan, *The Social Life of Coffee: The Emergence of the British Coffeehouse* (New Haven, CT: Yale University Press, 2005).

14. *An Account of the Fair Intellectual-Club in Edinburgh: In a Letter to a Honourable Member of an Athenian Society There* (Edinburgh: J. M'Euen, 1720).

15. Otto Dann, "Die Lesegesellschaften des 18. Jahrhunderts und der gesellschaftliche Aufbruch des deutschen Bürgertums," in *Buch und Leser*, ed. Herbert G. Göpfert (Hamburg: Hauswedell, 1977), 168.

16. Virginia Woolf, *To the Lighthouse*, ed. Stella McNichol (London: Penguin, 2000), 131–32.

17. Bertrand Badiou et al., eds., *Correspondence: Ingeborg Bachmann and Paul Celan*, trans. Wieland Hoban (London: Seagull Books, 2010), 137.

18. Readers interested in a good history of computing should see Georges Ifrah, *The Universal History of Computing*, trans. E. F. Harding (New York: John Wiley, 2000), and Atsushi Akera and Frederik Nebeker,

From 0 to 1: An Authoritative History of Modern Computing (New York: Oxford University Press, 2002).

19. Peter H. Salus, *A Quarter Century of Unix* (New York: Addison-Wesley, 1994), 65.

20. Fred Turner, *From Counterculture to Cyberculture: Stewart Brand, the Whole Earth Network, and the Rise of Digital Utopianism* (Chicago: Chicago University Press, 2006); Sam Williams, *Free as in Freedom: Richard Stallman's Crusade for Free Software* (Sebastopol, CA: O'Reilly, 2002); and Adrian Johns's location of the openness of hacker culture in the tradition of pirate radio. Adrian Johns, *Piracy: The Intellectual Property Wars from Gutenberg to Gates* (Chicago: University of Chicago Press, 2009), 357–400 and 463–96.

21. Antoine Hennion, "Those Things That Hold Us Together: Taste and Sociology," *Cultural Sociology* 1, no. 1 (2007): 103.

22. Henry Jenkins, *Convergence Culture: Where Old and New Media Collide* (New York: New York University Press, 2006), 4.

23. On "wreading," see Michael Joyce, "Nonce upon Some Times: Re-reading Hypertext Fiction," *Modern Fiction Studies* 43, no. 3 (Fall 1997): 579–97; and on "produsage," see Axel Bruns, *Blogs, Wikipedia, Second Life, and Beyond: From Production to Produsage* (New York: Peter Lang Publishing, 2008).

24. Andrew Keen, *Digital Vertigo: An Anti-Social Manifesto* (New York: St. Martin's, 2012); Susan Cain, *Quiet: The Power of Introverts in a World That Can't Stop Talking* (New York: Crown, 2012); Sven Birkerts, "The Room and the Elephant," *Los Angeles Review of Books*, June 7, 2011.

25. G. Post, K. Giocarinis, and R. Kay, "The Medieval Heritage of a Humanist Ideal: 'Scientia Donum Dei est, Unde Vendi non Potest,'" *Traditio* 11 (1955): 195–234.

26. Ray Kurzweil, *The Singularity Is Near: When Humans Transcend Biology* (New York: Viking, 2005). For reflections on the unity of technological consciousness, see Kevin Kelly, *What Technology Wants* (New York: Viking, 2010).

27. *The Athenaeum*, no. 22 (April 8, 1828): 335. I am indebted to Jon Klancher, *The Making of English Reading Audiences, 1790–1832* (Madison: University of Wisconsin Press, 1987), 60, for this reference.

28. James Boyle, "A Politics of Intellectual Property: Environmentalism for the Net?," *Duke Law Journal* 47, no. 1 (1998): 87–116.

29. Adrian Johns, *Piracy*, 497–518. For someone with such a capacious

view of the history of IP, we need to take Johns's argument very seriously.

30. See Bill Maurer and Gabriele Schwab, eds., *Accelerating Possessions: Global Futures of Property and Personhood* (New York: Columbia University Press, 2006). For Jaron Lanier, the myth of open source is a means of disempowering a creative middle class. When creative content is free, only the few who aggregate content and sell advertising through aggregation are the ones who make money in this new system. Google, Facebook, and YouTube make the money, not the individuals who make the content. Jaron Lanier, *You Are Not a Gadget* (New York: Knopf, 2010).

31. For a critique of the Creative Commons along these lines, see David Berry and Giles Moss, "On the 'Creative Commons': A Critique of the Commons without Commonality," *Free Software Magazine*, no. 5 (June 2005): http://www.freesoftwaremagazine.com/articles/commons_without_commonality. For Brandeis's decision on ideas as being common as air, see International News Service v. Associated Press, 248 US 215, 250 (1918). For an updated explication of this idea, see Lewis Hyde's *Common as Air: Revolution, Art, and Ownership* (New York: Farrar, Strauss, and Giroux, 2010).

32. Leigh Hunt, "Pocket-Books and Keepsakes," in *The Keepsake* (London: Hurst, Chance & Co., 1828), 17.

33. Ralph Waldo Emerson, "Friendship," 126.

34. Walter Benjamin, "Unpacking My Library," *Selected Writings*, vol. 2.2, ed. Michael W. Jennings, Gary Smith, and Howard Eiland (Cambridge, MA: Harvard University, 2005), 486–93.

35. David Cressy, "Books as Totems in Seventeenth-Century England and New England," *History of the Book in the West: 1455–1700*, vol. 2, ed. Ian Gadd (Burlington, VT: Ashgate, 2010), 502.

36. See Isaac Mao's manifesto that emerged from Ars Electronica 2009, in which he describes cloud computing as "a vast social brain in which every Internet user is a metaphorical neuron." Isaac Mao, "Cloud Intelligence," *Human Nature*, ed. Gerfried Stocker and Christine Schopf (Ostfildern: Hatje Cantz, 2010), 21.

37. Mimi Zeiger, "Only Collect," *Domus*, February 23, 2011, http://www.domusweb.it/en/op-ed/only-collect/. See also the thoughtful reflection by Frank Chimero on the nature of digital sharing of found objects: http://blog.frankchimero.com/post/5427297332, as well as his "dialogical" blog: http://www.themavenist.org/.

CHAPTER 6

1. Alfred Kelletat, ed., *Der Göttinger Hain* (Stuttgart: Reclam, 1967).

2. John Keats, "Endymion," in *Complete Poems and Selected Letters of John Keats* (New York: Modern Library, 2001), book 1, lines 460–61.

3. Manuel Joaquim Silva Pinto, "Investigating Information in the Multi-screen Society: An Ecologic Perspective," *Digital Literacy: Tools and Methodologies for the Information Society*, ed. Pier Cesare Rivoltella (Hershey, PA: IGI, 2008), 207–16.

4. For the definitive study on the representation of reading, see Garrett Stewart, *The Look of Reading: Book, Painting, Text* (Chicago: University of Chicago Press, 2006).

5. Gaston Bachelard, *The Poetics of Space*, trans. Maria Jolas (Boston: Beacon Press, 1994), 137.

6. In addition to Bachelard, the classic treatment on this topic is Susan Stewart, *On Longing: Narratives of the Miniature, the Gigantic, the Souvenir, the Collection* (Baltimore: Johns Hopkins University Press, 1984). On miniature books, see Louis W. Bondy, *Miniature Books: Their History from the Beginnings to the Present Day* (London: Sheppard Press, 1981), and Anne C. Bromer and Julian I. Edison, *Miniature Books: 4,000 Years of Tiny Treasures* (New York: Grolier Club, 2007).

7. Gaston Bachelard, *The Poetics of Space*, 155.

8. As the character Thomas Abrams from *The Rings of Saturn* remarks on his making a miniature of the Temple of Jerusalem: "Now, as the edges of my field of vision are beginning to darken, I sometimes wonder if I will ever finish the Temple and whether all I have done so far has not been a wretched waste of time. But on other days, when the evening light streams in through this window and I allow myself to be taken in by the overall view I see for a moment . . . as if everything were already completed and as if I were gazing into eternity." W. G. Sebald, *The Rings of Saturn*, trans. Michael Hulse (New York: New Directions, 1998), 248.

9. Toni Morrison, *Paradise* (New York: Knopf, 1997), 306.

10. The history of the relationship between reading and work is largely untold at the moment. For an excellent discussion of the way reading, and in particular rereading, was integrated within the rhythms of everyday productive life in the nineteenth century, the way it was

made "workable," see Deirdre Lynch, "Canon's Clockwork: Novels for Everyday Use," in *Bookish Histories: Books, Literature, and Commercial Modernity, 1700–1900*, ed. Ina Ferris and Paul Keen (Basingstoke: Palgrave Macmillan, 2009), 87–110.

11. Erich Schön, *Der Verlust der Sinnlichkeit* (Stuttgart: Klett-Cotta, 1987), 63–72.

12. Edgar Allan Poe, "Philosophy of Furniture," in *The Short Fiction of Edgar Allan Poe: An Annotated Edition*, ed. Stuart Levine and Susan Levin (Champaign: University of Illinois Press, 1990), 17.

13. Charles Baudelaire, *Parisian Scenes*, in *Complete Poems*, trans. Walter Martin (Manchester: Carcanet, 2006), 235; Thomas De Quincey, *Confessions of an English Opium-Eater*, ed. Joel Faflak (Peterborough: Broadview, 2009), 98–99.

14. Siegfried Kracauer, *Straßen in Berlin und anderswo* (Frankfurt am Main: Suhrkamp, 1964), 10.

15. The classic work on zines is Stephen Duncombe, *Notes from Underground: Zines and the Politics of Alternative Culture* (New York: Verso, 1997).

16. For a discussion, see Justin Stagl, *A History of Curiosity: The Theory of Travel, 1550–1800* (Chur, Switzerland: Harwood Academic Publishers, 1995).

17. See J. W. Goethe, *Italian Journey*, trans. W. H. Auden and Elizabeth Mayer (New York: Schocken, 1962), 134.

18. For a great example of this practice in action, see Lisa Jardine and Anthony Grafton, "'Studied for Action': How Gabriel Harvey Read His Livy," in *The History of the Book in the West: 1455–1700*, ed. Ian Gadd (Burlington, VT: Ashgate, 2010), 451–99.

19. Charles J. Woodbury, *Talks with Ralph Waldo Emerson* (New York: Baker and Taylor, 1890), 27

20. Roland Barthes, *The Pleasure of the Text*, trans. Richard Miller (New York: Hill and Wang, 1975), 31. For one of the best-known discussions of fragmentary reading as a form of "poaching," see Michel de Certeau, "Reading as Poaching," in *The Practice of Everyday Life*, trans. Steven F. Rendall (Berkeley: University of California Press, 1984), 165–76. For a discussion of such practices in the early modern period, see Peter Stallybrass, "Books and Scrolls: Navigating the Bible," in *Books and Readers in Early Modern England*, ed. Jennifer Andersen and Elizabeth Sauer (Philadelphia: University of Penn-

sylvania Press, 2002), 42–79. For the nineteenth century, see Leah Price, *The Anthology and the Rise of the Novel: From Richardson to George Eliot* (Cambridge: Cambridge University Press, 2000).

21. Henry Petroski, *The Book on the Bookshelf* (New York: Knopf, 1999).

22. Jean-Paul Sartre, *The Words*, trans. Bernard Frechtman (New York: Vintage, 1981), 40.

23. Pervasive or ubiquitous computing seeks to locate models of "continuous interaction," which "leverage" our interactions with the world, moving computing "off the desktop" and into "natural interfaces." In this, pervasive computing is both deeply spatially aware, but also aims to become a kind of computational unconscious, so that it runs in our mental and experiential "background." See Gregory D. Abowd and Elizabeth D. Mynatt, "Charting Past, Present and Future Research in Ubiquitous Computing," *ACM Transactions on Computer-Human Interaction* 7, no. 1 (2000): 29–58. As the editors of the volume *Small Tech* write, "The next wave of new media studies will need to examine the ecological interrelationships among the virtual space of the Internet, the enclosed space of the installation, and the open space of everyday life." Byron Hawk, David M. Rieder, and Ollie Oviedo, eds. *Small Tech: The Culture of Digital Tools* (Minneapolis: University of Minnesota Press, 2008), ix. See also Malcolm McCullough, *Digital Ground: Architecture, Pervasive Computing, and Environmental Knowing* (Cambridge, MA: MIT Press, 2004).

24. For a useful introduction to the field, see Jörgen Schäfer and Peter Gendolla, eds., *Beyond the Screen: Transformations of Literary Structures, Interfaces and Genres* (Bielefeld: Transcript, 2010), and the "Special Issue on Locative Media," ed. Drew Hemment, *Leonardo Electronic Almanac* 4, no. 3 (2006).

25. As the editors would write of the "Newsmonger" in *The Tatler* in 1710: "He had a Wife and several Children; but was much more inquisitive to know what passes in *Poland* than his own family . . . When I asked him whether he had yet married his eldest Daughter? He told me, No. But pray, says he, tell me sincerely, What are your Thoughts of the King of *Sweden*?" *The Commerce of Everyday Life: Selections from The Tatler and The Spectator*, ed. Erin Mackie (New York: Bedford/St. Martin's, 1998), 59.

26. Ted Nelson, "Computer Lib/Dream Machines," *The New Media*

Reader, ed. Noah Wardrip-Fruin and Nick Montfort (Cambridge, MA: MIT Press, 2003), 301–38.

27. Giselle Beiguelman, "Egoscope": http://desvirtual.com/egoscopio/english/about.htm.

28. http://about.nonchalance.com/philosophy.php.

29. Fan Di'An and Zhang Ga, *Synthetic Times: Media, Art, China* (Cambridge, MA: MIT Press, 2008).

30. There are a number of new media works that take the tree as their conceptual starting point. See Anne France Wysocki's beautiful animated text *Leaved Life* (2005), or Eduardo Kac's mind-warping bioart, *Natural History of the Enigma* (2009), which melds his DNA with a plant he calls an "Edunia." The text here produces a leaf that is also part human, taking Goethe's book-inspired invocation, "All is leaf," to a entirely new level.

31. The most exhaustive treatment of this idea occurs in the work of the German sociologist Niklas Luhmann, whose corpus is dedicated to illustrating the intellectual and social consequences of moving from a hierarchically organized society (of trees) to one based on "functional differentiation" (of fields). For an introduction, see Niklas Luhmann, *Social Systems,* trans. John Bednarz Jr. with Dirk Baecker (Stanford, CA: Stanford University Press, 1995).

32. See Chad Wellmon and Brad Pasanek, "The Bibliographic Enlightenment" (forthcoming).

33. For Descartes, the plane was the ideal space of rational knowledge. For Friedrich Schiller, the plane marked the beginning of human history recounted in his elegy, "The Walk" (1795). For the twentieth-century philosopher Martin Heidegger, the "clearing" signaled the beginning of becoming human, and for the postmodern philosophers Gilles Deleuze and Félix Guattari, the unbounded plane was refined into the "plateau" as the new ideal form of knowledge. The plane persists as one of reason's primal scenes.

34. Robert Pogue Harrison, *Forests: The Shadow of Civilization* (Chicago: University of Chicago Press, 1992), 100.

35. New library projects have been featured as showcases of urban as well as civic renewal in cities such as Seattle, Montreal, and Manchester, England. For a discussion, see Shannon Mattern, *The New Downtown Library: Designing with Communities* (Minneapolis: University of Minnesota Press, 2007).

36. According to the American Booksellers Association, membership of independent bookstores has increased 25 percent since 2005. For examples of new bookstores, see Ooga Booga in Los Angeles, Word in Brooklyn, or the self-publishing pop-up store Blurb in New York. Of course, these won't last, but that is largely the point—to imagine more provisional, recessed, and materially fluid ways of interacting with books.

37. Jeff Greenwald, "Long Overdue, the Bookmobile Is Back," *Smithsonian Magazine*, February 23, 2011, http://www.smithsonianmag .com/arts-culture/Long-Overdue-The-Bookmobile-Is-Back.html.

38. This term is inspired by Alan Liu's idea of the data "pour" to describe the nature of reading online—the way data is poured into the reader's view, but is never permanent, like water. The data "pore," on the other hand, is a way of thinking about the holes in networks, the places where our reading is *not* measurable, where we can intellectually "breathe."

CHAPTER 7

1. For an introduction to the history of writing, see Steven Roger Fischer, *A History of Writing* (London: Reaktion Books, 2001).

2. As N. Katherine Hayles writes, "electronic text is a process not an object." N. Katherine Hayles, "Translating Media," in *My Mother Was a Computer: Digital Subjects and Literary Texts* (Chicago: University of Chicago Press, 2005), 101.

3. David Golumbia, *The Cultural Logic of Computation* (Cambridge, MA: Harvard University Press, 2009). An important forerunner of this critique can be found in the work of the phenomenologist Edmund Husserl, *The Crisis of European Sciences and Transcendental Philosophy*, trans. David Carr (Evanston, IL: Northwestern University Press, 1970). See also Friedrich Kittler who speaks hyperbolically of "the 2000 year-old war between algorithms and alphabets." Friedrich Kittler, *Optical Media*, trans. Anthony Enns (Cambridge: Polity, 2010), 230.

4. For an introduction to the major works in the field, see Espen Aarseth, *Cybertext: Perspectives on Ergodic Literature* (Baltimore: Johns Hopkins University Press, 1997); Ian Bogost, *Unit Operations: An Approach to Video Game Criticism* (Cambridge, MA: MIT Press,

2006); Jesper Juul, *Half Real: Video Games between Real Rules and Fictional Worlds* (Cambridge, MA: MIT Press, 2005); Alexander R. Galloway, *Gaming: Essays on Algorithmic Culture* (Minneapolis: University of Minnesota Press, 2006); Steven E. Jones, *The Meaning of Video Games: Gaming and Textual Strategies* (New York: Routledge, 2008); and Noah Wardrip-Fruin, *Expressive Processing: Digital Fictions, Computer Games, Software Studies* (Cambridge, MA: MIT Press, 2009).

5. Jane McGonigal, *Reality Is Broken: Why Games Make Us Better and How They Can Change the World* (New York: Penguin, 2011), 354.

6. The classic work is Johan Huizinga, *Homo Ludens: A Study of the Play Element in Culture* (New York: Harper Row, 1970). See also Friedrich Schiller, *On the Aesthetic Education of Man*, trans. Elizabeth M. Wilkinson and L. A. Willoughby (Oxford: Clarendon Press, 1967), 107.

7. Northrop Frye, *Anatomy of Criticism* (Princeton, NJ: Princeton University Press, 1957), 280. For a brilliant reflection on how the riddle has served as a means of understanding the nature of things, see Daniel Tiffany, "Lyric Substance: On Riddles, Materialism, and Poetic Obscurity," *Critical Inquiry* 28, no. 1 (2001): 72–98.

8. Archer Taylor, *The Literary Riddle before 1600* (Berkeley: University of California Press, 1948); Tomas Tomasek, *Das deutsche Rätsel im Mittelalter* (Tübingen: Niemeyer, 1994); and Bruno Roy, *Devinettes françaises du moyen âge* (Montreal: Bellarmin, 1977).

9. André Jolles, *Einfache Formen* (Tübingen: Niemeyer, 1968), 135.

10. Anthony Bonner, ed., *Selected Works of Ramon Llull*, vol. 1 (Princeton, NJ: Princeton University Press, 1985), 579. For a discussion of the history of such algorithmic devices, see David Link, "Scrambling T-R-U-T-H: Rotating Letters as a Material Form of Thought," *Variantology* 4 (2010): 215–66.

11. Georg Philipp Harsdörffer, *Deliciae Physico-Mathematicae, oder, Mathematische und Philosophische Erquickstunden* (Nuremberg: Dümler, 1651). For an excellent discussion of Harsdörffer's ring, see Whitney Trettien, "Computers, Cut-Ups, and Combinatory Volvelles: An Archaelogy of Text-Generating Mechanisms," http://whitneyannetrettien.com/thesis/.

12. Henry Carrington Bolton, *The Counting-Out Rhymes of Children:*

Their Antiquity, Origin and Wide Distribution (New York: D. Appleton, 1888).

13. Dawn Addes, ed., *The Dada Reader* (London: Tate Publishing, 2006), 119.

14. Dawn Addes, *The Dada Reader*, 37.

15. Alan Turing, "On Computable Numbers, with an Application to the Entscheidungsproblem (1936)," in *The Essential Turing*, ed. B. Jack Copeland (Oxford: Clarendon, 2004), 75.

16. David Berlinski, *The Advent of the Algorithm: The Idea That Rules the World* (New York: Harcourt, 2000), xvi.

17. For a critique of our overreliance on Google search, see Siva Vaidhyanathan, *The Googlization of Everything (And Why We Should Worry)* (Berkeley: University of California Press, 2011), and John Battelle, *The Search: How Google and Its Rivals Rewrote the Rules of Business and Transformed Our Culture* (New York: Portfolio, 2005).

18. Noah Wardrip-Fruin, "Playable Media and Textual Instruments," *Dichtung Digital* 1 (2005): http://dichtung-digital.org/2005/1/Wardrip-Fruin/, and Kenneth Goldsmith, *Uncreative Writing* (New York: Columbia University Press, 2011). For a regularly updated review of new algorithmically driven authoring programs, see Judy Malloy, ed., *Application Software for Electronic Literature and New Media*: http://www.narrabase.net/.

19. J. W. Goethe, *Torquato Tasso*, in *Plays*, trans. Charles E. Passage (New York: Continuum, 1993), 241.

20. Virginia Woolf, *To the Lighthouse*, ed. Stella McNichol (London: Penguin, 2000), 131.

21. *Apostrophe*, compiled by Bill Kennedy and Darren Wershler (Toronto: ECW Press, 2006).

22. As Cayley writes, "My intention has been, in part, to interrogate certain relationships between the granular or atomic structures of alphabetically transcribed language and the critically or interpretatively discoverable rhetorical and aesthetic effects of literature." John Cayley, "Overboard: An Example of Time-Based Poetics in Digital Art," *Dichtung Digital* 32, no. 2 (2004): http://www.dichtung-digital .org/2004/2-Cayley.htm.

23. For a review, see Michele White, "The Aesthetic of Failure," in *The Body and the Screen: Theories of Internet Spectatorship* (Cambridge, MA: MIT Press, 2006), 85–114.

24. Digital humanities is a capacious term that encompasses a number of practices including the creation of multimedia archives, open-source publishing, virtual research environments, geographic mapping of cultural material, and the quantitative analysis of music, images, and text. My discussion here will be limited to how quantitative analysis impacts the way we read. For an introduction to the field, see Matthew Kirschenbaum, "What Is Digital Humanities and What's It Doing in English Departments?," *ADE Bulletin* 150 (2010): 55–61, and Susan Schreibman, Raymond George Siemens, and John Unsworth, eds., *A Companion to Digital Humanities* (Malden, MA: Blackwell, 2004).

25. Tanya Clement, "'A thing not beginning and not ending': Using Digital Tools to Distant-Read Gertrude Stein's *The Making of Americans*," *Literary and Linguistic Computing* 23, no. 3 (2008): 361–81. FeatureLens is one of many analytical tools that are currently in development, such as Stéfan Sinclair's Voyeur or the suite of applications available through academic consortia like Tapor, INK-E, or Philologic.

26. John W. Mohr and Vincent Duquenne, "The Duality of Culture and Practice: Poverty Relief in New York City, 1888–1917," *Theory and Society* 26, no. 2/3 (1997): 305–56.

27. See Andrew Piper, "Reading's Refrain: From Bibliography to Topology," *Reading: Selected Essays from the English Institute*, ed. Joseph Slaughter (Cambridge, MA: English Institute in Collaboration with the American Council of Learned Societies, forthcoming), and Andrew Piper and Mark Algee-Hewitt, "The Werther Effect," in *Distant Readings/Descriptive Turns: Topologies of German Culture in the Long Nineteenth Century* (Rochester, NY: Camden House, forthcoming).

28. See the foundational study of *Werther*'s influence, Klaus Scherpe, *Werther und Wertherwirkung: Zum Syndrom bürgerlicher Gesellschaftsordnung im 18. Jahrhundert* (Bad Homburg: Gehlen, 1970).

29. The term has been popularized by Franco Moretti, *Graphs, Maps, and Trees: Abstract Models for a Literary History* (London: Verso, 2007). The practices of distant reading are actually quite common to the older work of stylistics or authorship attribution, where statistical techniques of reading have proven very successful at identifying to whom unknown works belong, still an important feature used today

in trying to determine how documents are alike. The turn to using the term "distant reading" is a way of capturing a new interest in questions of scale.

30. Indeed, such interfaces take us all the way back to the form of the list itself, one of the most elementary types of reading (and of course adding). See Lucie Dolezalová, ed., *The Charm of a List: From the Sumerians to Computerised Data Processing* (Cambridge: Cambridge Scholars Publishing, 2009); Umberto Eco, *The Infinity of Lists* (Paris: Musée du Louvre/Rizzoli, 2009); Robert E. Belknap, *The List: The Uses and Pleasures of Cataloguing* (New Haven, CT: Yale University Press, 2004).

31. For his discussion of the importance of repetition and the refrain in the making of "The Raven," see E. A. Poe, "The Philosophy of Composition," in *Essays and Reviews*, ed. G. R. Thompson (New York: Library of America, 1984), 13–25.

32. Friedrich Schleiermacher, *Hermeneutik und Kritik*, ed. Manfred Frank (Frankfurt am Main: Suhrkamp, 1977), 218.

33. See Anthony Grafton and Megan Williams, *Christianity and the Transformation of the Book: Origen, Eusebius, and the Library of Caesarea* (Cambridge, MA: Belknap Press, 2006).

34. See Sebastiano Timpanaro, *The Genesis of Lachmann's Method*, ed. and trans. Glen W. Most (Chicago: Chicago University Press, 2005), and my work on the history of the critical edition, Andrew Piper, *Dreaming in Books: The Making of the Bibliographic Imagination in the Romantic Age* (Chicago: University of Chicago Press, 2009), 85–120.

35. Stéfan Sinclair, Stan Ruecker, and Peter Organisciak, "Ubiquitous Text Analysis," *Poetess Archive Journal* 2, no. 1 (2010): http://paj .muohio.edu/paj/index.php/paj/article/view/13.

36. On global literacy rates, see *Human Development Report 2009: Published for the United Nations Development Programme* (New York: Palgrave Macmillan, 2009), 171–75. On disability and education in the United States, see Thomas D. Snyder and Sally A. Dillow, *Digest of Education Statistics 2010* (Washington, DC: National Center for Education Statistics, Institute of Education Sciences, US Department of Education, 2011). On adult functional literacy, see *Reach Higher, America: Report of the National Commission on Adult Literacy* (Washington, DC: Council for Advancement of Adult Literacy, 2008).

EPILOGUE

1. Jean Paul, *Flegeljahre* (Stuttgart: Reclam, 1994), 127.
2. Stéphane Mallarmé, "The Book: A Spiritual Instrument," in *Selected Prose Poems, Essays, and Letters*, trans. Bradford Cook (Baltimore: Johns Hopkins University Press, 1956), 24.
3. For a thorough review of the entire field of book art, see Garrett Stewart, *Bookwork: Medium to Object to Concept to Art* (Chicago: University of Chicago Press, 2011). For a history of the destruction of books, see Fernando Báez, *A Universal History of the Destruction of Books: From Ancient Sumer to Modern Iraq*, trans. Alfred MacAdam (New York: Atlas, 2008).
4. Johann Georg Hamann, *Briefwechsel*, ed. Walther Ziesemer, vol. 4 (Wiesbaden: Insel, 1956), 401, 376.
5. Robert Burton, *The Anatomy of Melancholy* (New York: New York Review Books, 2001), 305.
6. Robert Burton, *The Anatomy of Melancholy*, 301.
7. Walter J. Ong, *Orality and Literacy: The Technologizing of the Word* (New York: Routledge, 2005), 40–41.
8. For the importance of redundancy, see the founding work of communication theory, Claude Shannon, *The Mathematical Theory of Communication* (Urbana: University of Illinois Press, 1964), and more recently, Jack P. Hailman, *Coding and Redundancy: Man-Made and Animal Evolved Signals* (Cambridge: Harvard University Press, 2008). For the significance of informational redundancy to the field of genetics, see Donald R. Forsdyke, *Evolutionary Bioinformatics*, 2nd ed. (New York: Springer, 2011).
9. *Briefe von Alexander von Humboldt an Varnhagen von Ense* (Leipzig: Brockhaus, 1860), 20.
10. See Susan Dalton, Nikola von Merveldt, Tom Mole, and Andrew Piper, et al., *Interacting with Print: Cultural Practices of Intermediality, 1700–1900* (forthcoming).
11. Victor Hugo famously created a scene in his novel *Notre-Dame de Paris* (1832) in which an observer points first at a book and then at a church and says, "This will kill that." Victor Hugo, *Notre-Dame de Paris*, trans. Alban Krailsheimer (Oxford: Oxford University Press, 2009), 190.